CHICAGO STADIUM

FRONT COVER: Hockey Hall of Famer Robert Marvin "Bobby" Hull (born January 3, 1939, in Point Anne, Ontario, Canada) joined the Chicago Black Hawks in 1957 at the age of 18. Nicknamed "the Golden Jet" because of his striking blonde hair and lightning speed on the ice, Hull led the team to the Stanley Cup in 1961. (Courtesy of author's collection.)

BACK COVER: A Curt Teich postcard dating to 1951 illustrates the sleek lines and Art Deco style of Chicago Stadium. (Courtesy of author's collection.)

COVER BACKGROUND: An exterior view of Chicago Stadium is pictured in the 1960s, the era that would produce four future Hall of Famers. (Courtesy of author's collection.)

CHICAGO STADIUM

Paul Michael Peterson

ISBN 978-0-7385-8307-5

Published by Arcadia Publishing
Charleston, South Carolina

Printed in the United States of America

Library of Congress Control Number: 2010939576

For all general information, please contact Arcadia Publishing:
Telephone 843-853-2070
Fax 843-853-0044
E-mail sales@arcadiapublishing.com
For customer service and orders:
Toll-Free 1-888-313-2665

Visit us on the Internet at www.arcadiapublishing.com

For the uncles Len, Wally, Ed, and Hube . . .
like the stadium, living in memories . . .

CONTENTS

ACKNOWLEDGMENTS

I imagine that fellow authors would agree with my statement that every finished book is a work in progress frozen in time by publication deadlines: there is always another paragraph one should have written, an additional quote one might have secured, and, in the case of this book, a hidden photograph one could have discovered. Research, however, is akin to the Greek rhetorical device *aposiopesis* in that it must ultimately trail off into silence when competing with the clock.

Thus, despite my desire to have included additional photographs and pages in this pictorial tome, I must pause to offer my thanks and good wishes to those who aided my journey with their patience, expertise, and encouragement. First and foremost, John Pearson and Jeff Ruetsche, both acquisition editors extraordinaire at Arcadia Publishing, who have guided me through four books to date; the research staff at the Library of Congress; Roy Kaltschmidt; Allan Janus and the Franklin D. Roosevelt Library in Hyde Park, New York; the Harry S. Truman Library in Independence, Missouri; Ruth Whitney, adjunct librarian at Oakton Community College in Des Plaines—who not only culled important source material but also endeavored to make research fun for me and my former writing students at Oakton; Diane, Louise, Melinda, and Nancy from the Department of Academic Success at Harper College in Palatine, all of whom add joy and good cheer to going to work each day (and eat the coffee cakes I bring); Keiko Kimura and the other "Keiksters" in AE/LS who support me professionally, and hopefully financially by purchasing this book; my wife, Joan, and my "little nuggets," Michael, Ryan, and William, whose unwavering love and support make me a better human being with each passing day.

Finally, and perhaps most importantly, my thanks to you, the reader, for your interest in this text. I fervently hope the contents of this book, while not exhaustive, offer you a nostalgic respite for that memorable sports palace fondly known as "the Madhouse on Madison."

A note to the reader: the Chicago Black Hawks spelled the team name consistently as two separate words until 1986, when the franchise initiated the change to "Blackhawks." Any sins of omission related to photographs, credits, or facts rest entirely with the responsibility of the author and were unintentional.

Unless noted otherwise, all images are courtesy of the author's collection.

INTRODUCTION

The neighborhoods on the West Side of Chicago were neither the best nor the worst in the city . . . For the most part, West Side neighborhoods remained outside the attention of other Chicagoans. They lacked the glamour of the emerging centers of commerce and wealth on the city's Near North Side and sections of the South Side. They were neither as lurid as the city's notorious vice district, the Levee, nor as promising as the lakefront park system planned by architect Daniel Burnham.

—Amanda Seligman
Block by Block: Neighborhoods and Public Policy on Chicago's West Side

"The house that Paddy built" . . . "the stadium" . . . "the Big Barn" . . . "the Madhouse on Madison" . . . Regardless of how fans through the decades have referred to Chicago Stadium, all of them can agree on one simple truth: the one-time structure located at 1800 West Madison Street was a lesson in the American dream. An elementary school dropout and the son of poor Irish emigrants realized a vision to build the greatest sports arena in the world. Men emigrated from other countries to play professional hockey on its ice, and, in the process, discovered a new home in the United States, professional success, and the undying adoration of fans who were legion. Franklin Delano Roosevelt, the 32nd president of the United States, pledged a "New Deal" under its roof, and four days before the American people would choose the 35th president, the nation's most powerful mayor pushed a young John F. Kennedy through a reported crowd of 30,000 that filled Chicago Stadium to the rafters and over the top of a national election. Boxing matches and circus performances entertained working men and women in the stadium's early years, while a young standout fresh from the University of North Carolina at Chapel Hill hypnotized the masses throughout the 1980s and 1990s, ultimately leading the Chicago Bulls to three consecutive National Basketball Association (NBA) championships in the stadium's final years.

The area framing the long-lost facade at 1800 West Madison Street was originally dotted by the slums and tenements that housed European emigrants in the late 19th and early 20th centuries. A little more than a generation afterward, in the late 1960s, the same area would play host to civil and racial unrest that repulsed those who witnessed its ill effects, driving many residents out of the city and into the waiting arms of nearby suburbs with the promise of a new American dream. And although new glory years lay ahead for the venue in the form of professional basketball and hockey, the aging Chicago Stadium began its inevitable decline as professional sports franchises nationwide began courting their athletes with newer, state-of-the-art facilities.

Today, a more modern 160-million-dollar athletic arena sits adjacent to the ground now occupied by a parking lot that, at one time, housed a 9.5-million-dollar sports palace. Small pockets of the surrounding neighborhood offer evidence of visible gentrification, but such progress will occur slowly and cautiously in a less optimistic economy. And while the occasional passersby and younger sports fans may have only heard of Chicago Stadium in stories passed down by previous generations, those who witnessed its glory and experienced its lessons in living the American dream in person can still hear the ringing of the fabled 3,633-pipe Barton organ and the echoing noise of crowds cheering loudly during the singing of the "National Anthem."

Remember the roar . . .

—Paul Michael Peterson
Chicago, August 2011

1

Harmon's Dream

It is not hard to please the public. All you have to do is remember that we are all born children, that we all die children, and that in between times we are children.

—Patrick T. "Paddy" Harmon
Chicago sports promoter and founder of the Chicago Stadium

In this 1927 image, Patrick T. "Paddy" Harmon (left) confers with Anton J. Cermak, then-president of the Cook County Board of Commissioners. Harmon was born in 1878 near Division and Halsted Streets to Irish emigrant parents from County Kerry. After dropping out of school at a young age, Harmon secured his education on the streets of Chicago and worked a variety of odd jobs to support his family before realizing success as one of the city's most highly respected dance-hall managers and sports promoters. Despite never having owned a major sports franchise, Harmon's vision of building the best sports arena in the world came to fruition with the construction of the Chicago Stadium as he financed $2.5 million of the project's reported cost of $7 million. Harmon was ultimately pushed out of the franchise, and, tragically, died penniless in an automobile accident 16 months after the stadium opened. Cermak later became mayor of Chicago and is viewed by history as the father of Chicago's "Democratic Machine." Ironically, both men were later honored with public funerals in Chicago Stadium. (Courtesy of *Chicago Daily News*.)

CHICAGO

claims the world's finest palace of sport — Chicago Stadium. This vast indoor amphitheater cost $7,000,000, and gives 25,000 people an unobstructed view of circus, rodeo, ice skating, bicycle racing, boxing and track events. *Edison Service* provides unfailing light and power for all provisions for comfort and enjoyment.

Commonwealth Edison Company

The Central Station Serving Chicago

Commonwealth Edison Company has paid 161 consecutive quarterly dividends. Send for Year Book. Stock listed on The Chicago Stock Exchange.

The city was proud of its new palace, and Commonwealth Edison took the opportunity, in this advertisement, to boast of its role in providing all light and power to Chicago Stadium.

A 1929 interior portrait of the Chicago Stadium depicts stadium founder Paddy Harmon (lower right) eyeing his young daughter Patsy, who stands upon the famous Barton organ as Mr. and Mrs. Ralph Waldo Emerson (no relation to the American author) look on. Emerson and his wife were staff organists at radio station WLS and appointed staff and assistant organists when the Chicago Stadium opened. (Courtesy of *Chicago Daily News*.)

Pictured above is a Curt Teich postcard of the Coliseum, the last of three indoor Chicago arenas bearing the same name. Built by candy magnate Charles F. Gunther, the Coliseum operated as a sports venue, convention center, and exhibition hall and was located on Wabash Avenue between Fourteenth and Sixteenth Streets. With a seating capacity of 6,000, the structure acted as precursor to the Chicago Stadium and hosted the Chicago Black Hawks from 1926 until 1929.

Construction for the stadium began in July 1928 on Chicago's Near West Side, with the actual work of wrecking buildings for the excavating crews initiating the stadium's birth. The nearby slums of the surrounding area were home to numerous European emigrants who were part of the mass migration to the United States in the late 19th and early 20th centuries. (Courtesy of *Chicago Daily News*.)

Built in 1927 with a capacity of 15,000, Detroit's Olympia Stadium, also known as the "Old Red Barn," was a model for Chicago Stadium. Detroit's sporting venue paralleled that of Chicago's in that it hosted rodeos, boxing matches, and concerts, in addition to housing the Detroit Red Wings of the National Hockey League (NHL) and the NBA's Detroit Pistons from 1957 until 1961. Neighborhood decline and the inevitable struggle against modernity led to the building's demise in September 1987.

New York's Madison Square Garden in its third incarnation was, at the time, the closest to Chicago Stadium in terms of capacity. It was built in 1925 and closed in 1968. In keeping with the competition between Chicago and New York, one Chicago newspaper article trumpeted its pride in Chicago's crowning achievement by writing, "And in its entirety it will shame New York's palatial Madison Square Garden."

Three months before the stadium opened in 1929, a *Chicago Daily Tribune* article from December 1928 reported on the continuing progress: "Accompanied by no more music than the rat-a-tat-tat of the riveter, Paddy Harmon's long projected stadium is moving from the dream stage into reality . . . In the block bounded by Madison, Wood, Warren, and Lincoln street an army of toilers is milling around in what to the man on the street appears to be a jungle of steel and timber." Pictured here is the progress of all that toil. (Courtesy of *Chicago Daily News*.)

When the last of the 12 trusses supporting the roof of the stadium was placed in position at the end of January 1929, it was said to be "one of the most difficult structural steel jobs ever erected in the United States." Each of the 12 trusses measured "266 feet in length, 28 feet in height, and 95 tons in weight." (Both courtesy of Library of Congress.)

A newspaper report at the time of the stadium's opening cited the following figures: "The building on the exterior will measure 300 by 266 feet . . . The 'flat,' or main floor, under which there has been no excavating, will measure 150 by 250 feet. The entire surface can be frozen for hockey or skating in four hours and defrosted in one hour." Additional available construction data included 398 million common bricks; 1.75 million face bricks; 3,700 tons of steel; 98,000 feet of one-and-a-quarter–inch pipe in the ice plant; and $40,000 worth of electric wire.

Pictured above and below is the famous Barton pipe organ. News reports heralded, "A pipe organ, the largest in the world and capable of producing volume equivalent to a 2,500 piece brass band, will call for $125,000. The units of the organ will be housed among the steel trusses. The keyboard will be so large that it will be upright and semicircular, so that one man can operate it." The brand-new pipe organ was built in 1929 by the Barton Organ Company of Oshkosh, Wisconsin. (Both courtesy of Library of Congress.)

The Curt Teich Company of Chicago operated from 1898 to 1978, producing landscape views and advertisement postcards. Pictured above is a night view of the completed stadium, while a daytime view graces the image below. A novel form of communication in an era decades away from e-mail, postcards were a popular way for travelers to share the sights with friends and family back home. Those who could not travel to see the stadium in person could at least acquire a paper souvenir of Chicago's Art Deco–inspired sports palace.

Four days prior to the opening of Chicago Stadium, Paddy Harmon offered the following quote to reporter Don Maxwell from the *Chicago Daily News*: "Everybody always said before I started anything that it couldn't be done. But Paddy did it. For three years I been trying to build this sports stadium. Twenty times I thought I had everything all set only to get knocked down. But I kept getting up, and next Thursday night the folks who said I couldn't are invited to come out on West Madison Street and see the building Paddy built."

2

A Dash of Hazard

Few sports beat hockey as a spectacle. The east sees a good deal of it. It is an important college and professional sport, with Canadians excelling in it. It will be a favorite hereabouts when it has been introduced, a game of speed with a sufficient dash of hazard.

—*Chicago Daily Tribune*, January 1, 1926

The National Hockey League marked its 10th season in 1926–1927 as Maj. Frederic McLaughlin purchased the Portland Rosebuds from the folding Western Hockey League. The now Chicago-based team became known as the Black Hawks, taking the ice on November 17, 1926, to claim a 4-1 victory against the Toronto St. Patrick's at the Chicago Coliseum. In less than three years, the new team would move to larger quarters at 1800 West Madison with the St. Patrick's Day opening of Chicago Stadium on March 28, 1929.

Maj. Frederic McLaughlin (holding the trophy) was the first owner and general manager of the Chicago Black Hawks hockey team. A former commander of the 333rd Machine-Gun Battalion of the 86th (Black Hawk) Infantry Division of the US Army and a wealthy coffee magnate, McLaughlin spent $12,000 to purchase his membership card in the National Hockey League after noting the popularity of Canadian hockey. He chose the name "Black Hawks" after his former army division. The Chicago Black Hawks were officially founded on September 25, 1926. McLaughlin led his franchise to two Stanley Cup wins, one in 1934, pictured here, and again in 1938.

Irene Castle (1893–1969), a famous ballroom dancer of the early 20th century, made Maj. Frederic McLaughlin her third husband and contributed her talents to her husband's franchise by designing the Black Hawks' famous, early logo of the Indian head and the shoulder patches with the crossed hockey sticks.

Clarence John "Taffy" Abel (1900–1964), pictured at right and below, was the first United States–born player to become a National Hockey League regular, playing in the NHL for eight years. Abel won a silver medal playing in the 1924 Winter Olympics before beginning his professional hockey career. He played for the Black Hawks for five seasons, from 1926–1927 to 1933–1934. (Both courtesy of *Chicago Daily News*.)

Merille Ernest Joseph "Ty" Arbour (1896–1979) played left wing for the Chicago Black Hawks for three seasons from 1927–1928 until 1930–1931. Arbour served in World War I from 1915 to 1918 before entering professional hockey. He served as a team captain for the Black Hawks and finished his career in the minors. (Courtesy of *Chicago Daily News*.)

Thomas John Cook (1907–1961) began his ice career as a forward in Canada, where he played 348 games in the National Hockey League. Cook was slight at just five feet and seven inches tall and 140 pounds, but he stood his ground against opponents, many of whom were considerably bigger in that era of hockey. He won the Stanley Cup in 1934 with the Chicago Black Hawks. (Courtesy of *Chicago Daily News*.)

Rosario "Lolo" Couture (1905–1986) began his NHL career as a 164-pound right wing with the Chicago Black Hawks in 1928, playing with them for seven years until the end of the 1935 season. Couture helped the Black Hawks win the Stanley Cup in 1934. (Courtesy of *Chicago Daily News.*)

Ted Edward Dixon "Teddy" Graham (1906–1979) was a professional ice hockey defenseman who played for the Chicago Black Hawks in 1927–1928, 1929–1930, and again from the 1930–1931 season until the 1932–1933 season, when he left Chicago to play for the Montreal Maroons. Born in Ontario, Canada, Graham stood 5 feet and 10 inches tall and weighed 175 pounds during his professional hockey years. (Courtesy of *Chicago Daily News.*)

John Gottselig (1906–1986) was the National Hockey League's first Russian-born player and, later, the first European-born coach in league history. He played left wing, joining the Black Hawks in 1928 after leaving the Regina Pats. In Gottselig's 17 seasons with the Black Hawks, he played in 589 games, scoring 176 goals and making 195 assists for 371 points. He helped lead the Hawks to the Stanley Cup in 1934 and 1938 (as team captain). He later coached the team for three years. Gottselig served as the Black Hawks' director of public relations in the early 1960s before leaving hockey for professional industry. (Both courtesy of *Chicago Daily News*.)

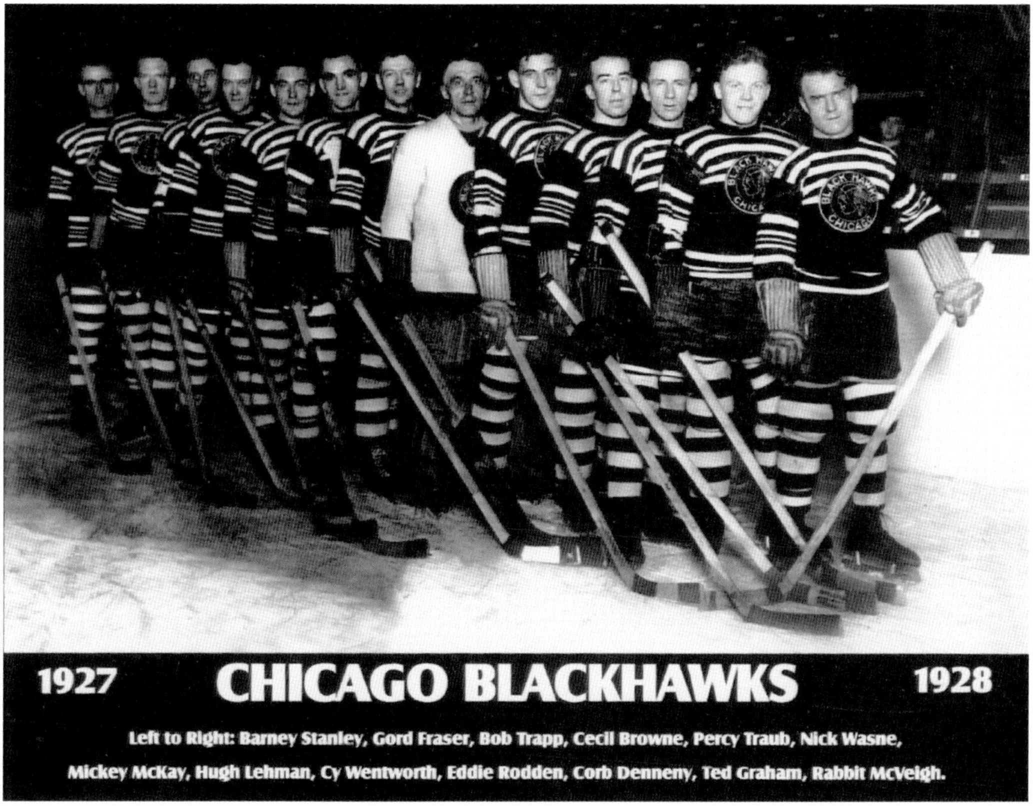
1927
CHICAGO BLACKHAWKS
1928
Left to Right: Barney Stanley, Gord Fraser, Bob Trapp, Cecil Browne, Percy Traub, Nick Wasne,
Mickey McKay, Hugh Lehman, Cy Wentworth, Eddie Rodden, Corb Denneny, Ted Graham, Rabbit McVeigh.

A 1927–1928 team photograph of the Black Hawks is pictured above. In their second season of play, Chicago would miss the play-offs for the first time in the club's short history, finishing 29 points behind the Pittsburgh Pirates for the final play-off spot in the American Division.

TAYLOR
BURNS
DUTKOWSKI
GARDINER
ABEL
COUTURE
INGRAM
ARBOUR
IRVIN
Coach
SHAUGHNESSY
Manager
DYER
Trainer
MILLER
1929 - 30 CHICAGO BLACKHAWKS HOCKEY TEAM
GOTTSELIG
COOK
MARCH
SOMERS
RIPLEY
WENTWORTH

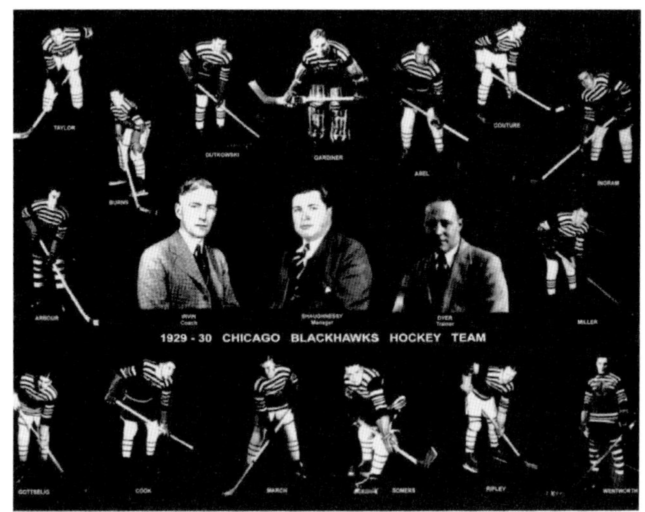

This image features the Chicago Black Hawks in 1929–1930, the team's fourth season in the National Hockey League. Interesting to note is that a disagreement with the Chicago Stadium Corporation resulted in the team playing at the Chicago Coliseum in November and December before the issue was resolved. The Hawks continued and completed the season in Chicago Stadium from December through March.

Pictured is Chicago Black Hawks coach Bill Stewart kissing the famed Stanley Cup in 1938. The 1938 Stanley Cup Finals was a best-of-five series between the Chicago Black Hawks and the Toronto Maple Leafs. Chicago won the series 3-1 to earn their second Stanley Cup.

A whimsical 1936 advertisement for Alfred Johnson Skate Company features Chicago Black Hawk players Johnny Gottselig and "Doc" Romnes. The company was well known for providing hockey outfits, skates, and shoes to the team.

In the 1937 image, Chicago Black Hawks player Earl Siebert confers with coach Clem Loughlin at the Hawks' stick rack located in the team's dressing room. In keeping with the "dash of hazard" theme, small blood stains dot the dressing room floor around Siebert. (Courtesy of *Chicago Daily News.*)

Here's a wintry view of Chicago Stadium during the era of those first Black Hawk teams.

3

LIONS, ICE SKATES, AND RODEOS

We can furnish anything in show business from a one man vaudeville to a three ring circus.

—United Amusement Company, 1934

Pictured above is Charles "Cowboy" Morgan Evans bulldogging at the Tex Austin Rodeo in Chicago Stadium in 1929. Evans, an American champion rodeo sports cowboy from Texas who worked as a rancher and oil drilling foreman, won the 1927 World Series Rodeo Bulldogging Championship at New York City's Madison Square Garden.

Thomas Patrick Loughran (1902–1982), at left (holding hat) with promoter Paddy Harmon and below training with a speed bag while Harmon watches, was the light heavyweight boxing champion of the world. Loughran, nicknamed the "Phantom of Philly," fought Mickey Walker in a bout at Chicago Stadium in the spring of 1929. (Both courtesy of *Chicago Daily News*.)

Ice Club of Chicago Plans Big 1936-37 Season

THE ICE CLUB of Chicago, a new organization to further the interests of figure skating, has leased the Chicago Stadium for a period of ten years. The Stadium will provide ice for the skaters on Sundays and two or three times a week, depending upon the dates of attractions using the Stadium. When the Black Hawks hockey team is in town and requires ice for practise there will be many many opportunities for members to get in extra sessions on the Stadium ice sheet.

• The Ice Club of Chicago has been voted a membership in the U. S. Figure Skating Association, the parent body of all similar skating clubs throughout the nation.

• Roy Shipstad and Bess Ehrhardt, two of the greatest professional stars in the figure skating world, who are well known to all Chicago ice fans because of their sensational skating in the Chicago Stadium Ice Carnival last winer, have been engaged as coaches and they will be assisted by a capable staff of instructors. There will be a special class for beginners.

• Membership in the club will be semi-exclusive in nature and applications must be submitted to the membership committee. Those wishing membership applications or information may address Thomas C. Worden, prominent Chicago business man, who is president of the club, in care of the Chicago Stadium. Membership dues are $15 for season, but in order to stimulate interest in pair figure skating a special rate of $20 per couple is offered. For $25 an entire family may be enrolled as members.

• Many features of a semi-social nature are planned for the coming winter at the Sunday skating sessions of the Ice Club of Chicago. Stars of hockey, luminaries of the figure skating world, professional and amateur, will be invited guests, and many novel entertainments are planned to round out the winter season of indoor skating. The Stadium has unrivaled facilities for these social skating parties.

Figure skating prefaced the popularity of professional hockey during the 1920s and 1930s. The advertisements on this page detail plans for the newly formed Ice Club of Chicago, in which anyone could pay for a membership to receive instruction from the biggest names in figure skating at that time.

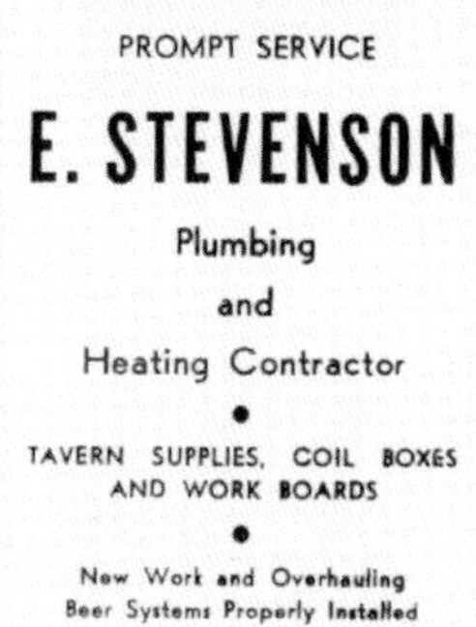

Western Blue Print
Company
Blue and Brown Line Prints
Photostats - Reproductions
Drawing Materials
North Side Shop
3529 No. Western Ave.
Lake View 1441-1442
West Side Shop
1212 So. Crawford Ave.
Lawndale 2516-2517
M. WOSKOW, Mgr. CHICAGO

CHICAGO • STADIUM

• THE WORLD'S FINEST STADIUM • WHETHER IT'S CIRCUS • CARNIVAL • OR COMPETITIVE SPORT • YOU ARE SURE OF A NIGHT OF THRILLS • YOU WILL NEVER REGRET THE MORNING AFTER IF YOU HAVE SPENT THE NIGHT BEFORE AT THE STADIUM •

MOTOR TROUBLE TONITE
PHONE SEELEY 9660
Brakes, Motor, Elec. Specialists
Brake Engineering Service
Victor Mustari, Mgr. Open All Night
2039 W. JACKSON BLVD.

HOTEL MARYLAND
RUSH AT DELAWARE
FAMOUS FOR ITS FOOD
LUNCHEON. 40c 50c 65c
DINNER . . . 65c 75c $1.00
HOME OF THE
CLOISTER INN TAVERN

Thirty-five

A whimsical advertisement for the Chicago Stadium from a 1936 program boasts that man does not live by hockey alone. "You will never regret the morning after if you have spent the night before at The Stadium" was a simple marketing pitch that today's admen would be proud to have written. Note the other advertisements of the era framing the stadium details.

John Henry Lewis

World's Light-Heavyweight Champion

vs. Red Burman

Jack Dempsey's Sensation

Wed. April 8th

4 - Other - 4 Heavyweight Fights

Chicago Stadium

No Raise in Prices

60c - $1.20 - $2.40

Tax Included

ORDER TICKETS NOW — On Sale at BOND'S, 65 W. Madison St., and the CHICAGO STADIUM GRILL, 1824 W. Madison St.

A boxing advertisement details a heavyweight bout scheduled at the stadium between John Henry Lewis and Red Burman. Note the no-nonsense prices in an age where pugilism ranked high among the top athletic events of the day. Lewis (1914–1974), an African American boxer, was the world light heavyweight champion from 1935 to 1939. Clarence "Red" Burman (1915–1996), a Baltimore native, later won distinction as a boxer in his 1941 bout with Joe Louis, another African American boxer of high fame.

A team photograph shows members of the 1933–1934 Chicago Black Hawks of Stanley Cup fame. In the 17th season of the National Hockey League, nine teams each played 48 games. The Chicago Black Hawks were the Stanley Cup winners after they beat the Detroit Red Wings three games to one. According to Joe Pelletier's website, "The Hawks experienced their lowest scoring NHL season in 1933–1934 and surprised everyone in the play-offs with their smothering defensive play and a few timely goals."

Hockey wasn't the only Chicago Stadium event played out on the ice. Pictured here are a cover and a page from the program of the Fourth Annual Mammoth International Ice Carnival that featured 23 different figure-skating events. Commenting on skating to the accompaniment of music in the program's introduction, Chicago Stadium organist Al Melgard wrote: "The Chicago Stadium Ice Carnival, now the foremost event of its kind in America, is the only great indoor figure skating ice show at which the music is supplied by the huge organ, instead of a band or orchestra. Other great stadiums and skating rinks are not equipped with organs. . . . Skating tempo is a bit faster than dance rhythm, as many will notice tonight in attending the Ice Carnival."

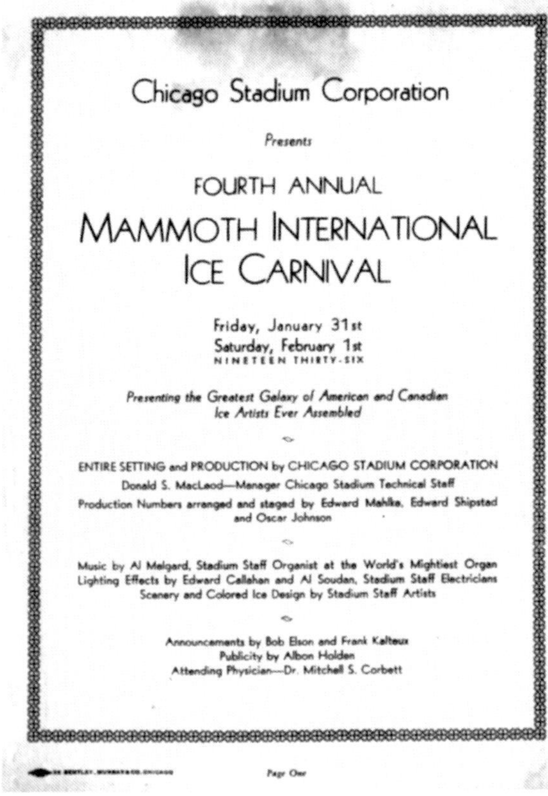

Chicago Stadium Corporation

Presents

FOURTH ANNUAL

MAMMOTH INTERNATIONAL
ICE CARNIVAL

Friday, January 31st
Saturday, February 1st
NINETEEN THIRTY-SIX

Presenting the Greatest Galaxy of American and Canadian Ice Artists Ever Assembled

ENTIRE SETTING and PRODUCTION by CHICAGO STADIUM CORPORATION
Donald S. MacLeod—Manager Chicago Stadium Technical Staff
Production Numbers arranged and staged by Edward Mahlke, Edward Shipstad and Oscar Johnson

Music by Al Melgard, Stadium Staff Organist at the World's Mightiest Organ
Lighting Effects by Edward Callahan and Al Soudan, Stadium Staff Electricians
Scenery and Colored Ice Design by Stadium Staff Artists

Announcements by Bob Elson and Frank Kalteux
Publicity by Albon Holden
Attending Physician—Dr. Mitchell S. Corbett

Page One

Pictured at right is a souvenir program cover of the Fourth Annual Mammoth International Ice Carnival in 1936. In a program article titled "Chicago Grows Skate Conscious," U.S. Olympic Skating Committee secretary Edward A. Mahlke wrote, "Chicago gets more skate conscious year by year. For many years Chicago produced more great speed skaters than any other city in the nation, but lagged far behind other cities in a general winter sports and skating program . . . we believe that the Carnival will further establish the Chicago Stadium show as America's premier indoor winter sport carnival. The Stadium Ice Carnival is here to stay as one of the colorful events of the whole year in sport entertainment." Below is a photograph showing throngs of patrons enjoying the Chicago Stadium program.

Queen of the Ice and 10-time world champion Sonja Henie is pictured above during one of her performances at the Chicago Stadium. This show marked Henie's third appearance in Chicago, for which she netted $200,000 over a few weeks for performances to sold-out crowds.

Pictured at right and below are programs for the Fourth Annual Mammoth International Ice Carnival. Discussing the burgeoning popularity of competitive figure skating and exhibition figure skating, Chicago sports reporter Albon Holden wrote at the time, "Chicago is famous as a center of recreational and pleasure skating. Pass any one of the dozens of park and playground lagoon ice rinks on a winter afternoon or evening when the thermometer is low enough to assure ice and you'll encounter huge crowds of enthusiastic skaters. I'll confess that during nearly twenty years as a Chicago sports writer I had never seen a big ice carnival . . . I just hadn't got the idea of what could be done in such an indoor arena as the Chicago Stadium in making the event a thrilling, glamorous, and delightful evening of entertainment."

CHICAGO STADIUM

SECOND EDITION OF

Fourth Annual Mammoth International Ice Carnival

April 2, 3, 4, 5 and Sat. Mat. April 4, 1936

PROGRAM OF EVENTS

1. CALL TO THE COLORS
   Salute to the Norwegian, British and American Flags
   Al Melgard at the Organ, Assisted by Trumpeteers
   Myrtale Campaninni, Vocalist
   Ruth Friedlund, Vocalist

2. "WINTER WALTZ"
   Introducing Complete Cast in Masquerade

3. GRACEFUL PAIR SKATING
   Harry Shipstad and Alyce McClellan of St. Paul

4. "AMERICA'S HOTCHA GIRL"
   Bess Ehrhardt of Superior, Wis.

5. GRANDMA WAIT
   A Demonstration of the Figure Skating Routine With Which She Won the 1876 Olympic Championship

6. "SQUADS RIGHT"
   Military Drill by the Sixteen Stadiumettes:

Vera Nelson	Peggy Maloney	Alvah Blade
Julie Finkleson	Betty Evanston	Grace Harvey
Genevieve Nelson	Marie Nelson	Dorothy Lewis
Naomi Wold	Jean Ryberg	Phyllis Rebholz
Peggy Foster	Jean Foster	
Laverne Busher	Virginia Nelson	

7. "APACHE DANCE"
   America's Most Sensational Skating Pair
   Everett McGowan and Ruth Mack

8. "UNCLE SAM BALANCING THE BUDGET"
   Featuring Johnnie Davidson of New York on Stilts

9. ATLANTIC CITY BOARD WALK BEAUTY CHAMPIONS
   Eddie Shipstad and Oscar Johnson

10. JACK DUNN
    British Figure Skate Champion in a Demonstration of His Famous Olympic Games Routine

11. AMERICA'S PREMIER FOUR
    The Nelson Sisters of Minneapolis

Ten

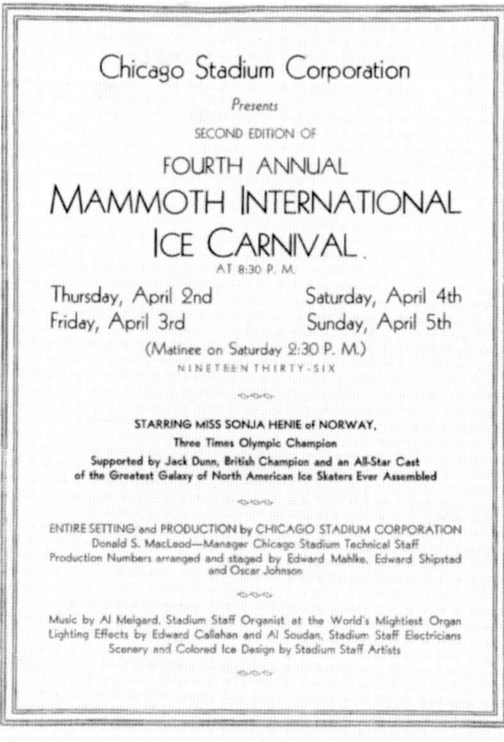

Chicago Stadium Corporation

Presents

SECOND EDITION OF

FOURTH ANNUAL

MAMMOTH INTERNATIONAL

ICE CARNIVAL

AT 8:30 P. M.

Thursday, April 2nd — Saturday, April 4th
Friday, April 3rd — Sunday, April 5th

(Matinee on Saturday 2:30 P. M.)

NINETEEN THIRTY-SIX

STARRING MISS SONJA HENIE of NORWAY,

Three Times Olympic Champion

Supported by Jack Dunn, British Champion and an All-Star Cast of the Greatest Galaxy of North American Ice Skaters Ever Assembled

ENTIRE SETTING and PRODUCTION by CHICAGO STADIUM CORPORATION
Donald S. MacLeod—Manager Chicago Stadium Technical Staff
Production Numbers arranged and staged by Edward Mahlke, Edward Shipstad and Oscar Johnson

Music by Al Melgard, Stadium Staff Organist at the World's Mightiest Organ
Lighting Effects by Edward Callahan and Al Soudan, Stadium Staff Electricians
Scenery and Colored Ice Design by Stadium Staff Artists

One

Genuine *DRAFT* Root Beer in Bottles!

★ **Looks Like Real Beer!** ★ **Pours Like Real Beer!**

★ **Aged & Mellowed!**

TRY A 12 Oz. "Junior" Size Bottle

•

SOLD HERE IN THE STADIUM

A real old fashioned taste-treat, perfect for every thirst occasion! Serve it at home at meal times and all through the day — enjoy it ANYWHERE in the handy 2-glass "Junior" size bottle! Insist on the genuine — ask for "Dad's" by name!

Tune In! TWO Outstanding "DAD'S" Radio Programs!
"RADIO NEWSREEL" WCFL Tues., Thur., Sat., 6:15 p.m.
"CAPTAIN DANGER" WMAQ Mon., Wed., Fri., 5:45 p.m.

2

For those fans who needed a refreshing drink while at the stadium, choices were myriad. A late-1930s program advertising two popular beverages praised the merits of Dad's Old Fashioned Draft Root Beer offered in three different "family" sizes.

And for those requiring something a little stronger, mellow and refreshing Meister Bräu or Patrick Henry beer were both sold and served in Chicago Stadium.

WHERE TO

Amusements

By Eric

HARRY'S NEW YORK CABARET

If you ask one hundred person the question: Which is the most talked of cabaret? The greater number would say Harry's New York Bar. It is the accepted nite club, famous here and abroad, for fine food and unusual entertainment. It is a well known fact that you will meet more socially prominent people at Harry's because it is the "accepted club of Chicago."

Dinner show at 8 P. M. Others 'til dawn. Private banquet room for all occasions, serving 25 to 350 persons. Phone Superior 8230 for information. Entire floor show furnished free.

• • •

THE TRADING POST

The Trading Post Restaurant at 108 East Oak Street is a unique place for dinner or late supper. Catering to a select public who appreciate the Continental type of food and entertainment, the management, under the direction of Colonel Wladimir Yaschenko, has created an atmosphere which is truly that of the old world.

• • •

BOB TOMLINSON

This school is a by-word among Chicago dance enthusiasts. They all agree that for beginners as well as for professionals this school is above the average in giving finished instructions. Bob Tomlinson teaches dancing in a way that you not only learn to dance but improves your posture and health.

• • •

WHITE HORSE CAFE

"Just a little better than the kind you thought best." That phrase is certainly applicable to the excellent cuisine and drinks served here. Be convinced. Drop in when leaving the Stadium, and let "Smiling Jensen" be your host for the evening. The music and entertainment are "tops."

Thirty-eight

Equally as important to one's enjoyment at Chicago Stadium was where to go afterwards. A late-1930s advertisement page details the many options available, from Ireland's Restaurant—"the favorite haunt for sea food loving Chicagoans"—to other venues featuring live floor shows for the more risqué of appetites.

Ice sports weren't the only action one could witness at Chicago Stadium, as evidenced by the 1937 World's Championship Rodeo souvenir program cover above. One essay detailing the history of Chicago's fascination with rodeos stated: "The first world's Championship Rodeo was held at the Chicago World's Fair in 1893 and was staged by none other than the historically famous character "Buffalo Bill" Cody. This portrayal of cowboy sports and pastimes met with unforeseen success and the public became highly enthused over the daring exhibitions of skill which were demonstrated by the hardy sons of the prairie."

CHICAGO STADIUM CORPORATION

PRESENTS THE

1937

WORLD'S CHAMPIONSHIP

R·O·D·E·O

$18,000 IN PURSES

October 14 to October 31

(Matinees Saturdays and Sundays)

Every Evening 8:30 P. M.

•

CHICAGO STADIUM CORPORATION RODEO
EXECUTIVE STAFF

James Norris .... *President*
Arthur M. Wirtz .... *Executive Vice-President and Treasurer*
James D. Norris .... *Executive Vice-President and Secretary*
Donald S. MacLeod .... *Manager*
Bob Hickey .... *Publicity*
W. E. "Candy" Hammer .... *Arena Director*
Lonnie Rooney .... *Asst. Arena Director*
Fred H. Kressmann .... *Arena Secretary*
Harry Greer .... *Supt. Live Stock*
Abe Lefton .... *Announcer*
Fred Beeson .... *Official Judge*
Shorty Ricker .... *Associate Judge*
Clay Carr .... *Associate Judge*

•

Barnes-Carruthers of Chicago .... *Associate Directors*

•

All Contest events under the Rules and Regulations of
RODEO ASSOCIATION OF AMERICA
Home Office, Salinas, Cal.

Although Chicago continued to hold rodeos even after the 1893 World's Fair, these exhibitions were not viewed as major events until Chicago Stadium began hosting this American sport. For those patrons without their own horse for getting to the stadium, the Chicago L accommodated one's transit needs, as shown in the advertisement below.

THE Rodeo is just one of the many outstanding events arranged for your pleasure by the Chicago Stadium throughout the season. They're all big-time attractions you'll not want to miss. And when you attend, remember that the one best way to get to and from the Stadium is by "L". No parking problems to solve, no traffic jams to fight. Saves you money, too. And you'll find service to and from the Madison Street "L" station (right at the Stadium) is fast and frequent, with direct connections to "L" trains to all parts of the city. Enjoy yourself more . . .

Ride the "L"

Pictured in this advertisement is the executive team behind the Chicago Stadium.

CHICAGO STADIUM CORPORATION

Presents

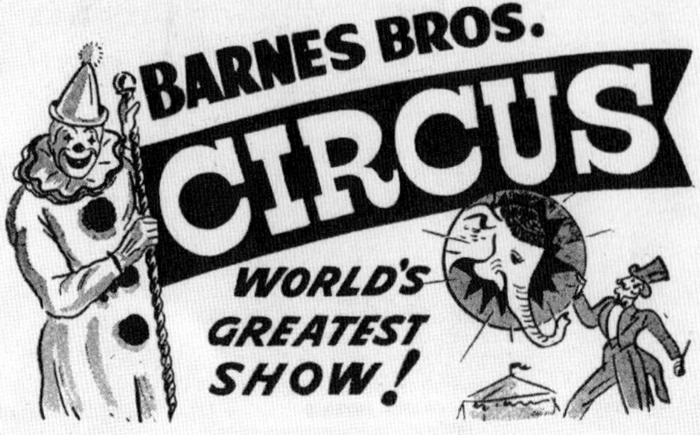

Friday, April 18th thru Sunday, May 11th

Nightly 8:30 P. M. **Matinee Daily 2:30 P. M.**

•

Children Half Price — All Performances Except Saturdays and Sundays

•

CHICAGO STADIUM CORPORATION — BARNES, CARRUTHERS, INC.
Associate Producers and Directors

STAFF FOR BARNES BROS. CIRCUS

ARTHUR M. WIRTZ - - - - - - - - - Executive Director
WM. H. BURKE - - - - - - - - - - - Production Director
SAM J. LEVY - - - - - - - - - - - - Production Manager

The "World's Greatest Show" captivated young and old alike at the Chicago Stadium, where many circus performances were held throughout the 1940s. Pictured above is a captivating image gracing the cover of a souvenir program for Barnes Bros. Circus. The origins of the circus as a means of entertainment date back to ancient Rome and Greece. Chariot racing and the exhibition of animals as traditional attractions in Greece inspired Rome to set up exhibitions featuring horse races, equestrian shows, staged battles, jugglers, and acrobats.

The circus performances headlined at Chicago Stadium offered two shows, including a daily matinee and an evening performance for up to three weeks. It is doubtless that Chicagoans were entranced by the international flavor of the events, as 1,000 performers and artists from Europe, Asia, and South America represented more than 100 acts.

The
CHICAGO STADIUM

PROUDLY PRESENTS
THE

"World's Greatest Show"

BARNES BROS.
CIRCUS

Produced By
CHICAGO STADIUM CORPORATION — BARNES - CARRUTHERS, INC.

April 22nd - May 8th

MATINEES 2:30 P. M. DAILY
EVENINGS 8:30 P. M.

STAFF FOR BARNES BROS. CIRCUS

ARTHUR M. WIRTZ . . . . . Executive Director
WM. H. BURKE . . . . . Production Director
SAM J. LEVY . . . . . Production Manager

... *Program* ...

FIFTEENTH ANNUAL

BARNES BROS. CIRCUS

FRIDAY, APRIL 18, thru SUNDAY, May 11, 1947 — Nightly 8:30 P.M. Matinees Daily at 2:30 P.M.

1. **A TRIP TO STORYBOOKLAND**
Staged and Devised by Marion MacDonald
Built by Modern Art Studio, Chicago, Illinois — Music and Lyrics by Marion MacDonald

	STAGE 1	CENTER RING	STAGE 2
2.		**ANTICS GALORE**	
	Hubert Dyer Co.	Ridola & Co.	The Hodgsons
		BARNES BROS. presents World's Largest Wild Animal Act Trained By	
3.		**THE PEER OF ALL WILD ANIMAL TRAINERS** Terrell Jacobs	
4.		**SKY - HI**	
	Ethel Marine		Three Franks
5.		**SPRINGTIME**	
	Clowns	Clowns	Clowns
6.		**CHINESE WONDER WORKERS**	
	Wong Brothers	Tien Tsi Lui Troupe	Canton Brothers
7.		**THE ACME OF EQUINE PERFECTION** Capt. William Heyer Presenting The Wonder Horse, "Starless Night"	
8.		**AERIAL BALLET** featuring Miss Elly Ardelty The Sensational Lady on the Flying Trapeze	
9.		**TONS OF FUN** BARNES BROTHERS Famous Elephants	
10.		**FANTASY OF JERX**	
	Clowns	Clowns	Clowns
11.		**QUEEN OF THE BOUNDING ROPE** The Incomparable La Tosca	
12.		**REVOLVING RYTHM** Three Franks	

The program of events lists acts headlining the Barnes Bros. Circus, which took Chicago Stadium by storm for three weeks in 1947. Stunning high-wire acts, wild animal trainers, and clowns hypnotized the audience in two shows each day.

:: PROGRAM :: Continued

SEVENTEENTH ANNUAL

BARNES BROS. CIRCUS

	STAGE 1	CENTER RING	STAGE 2
14.		**ALICE IN THE ENCHANTED FOREST** Staged and Devised by Marian MacDonald - Built by Modern Art Studios Music and Lyrics by Marian MacDonald	
15.	Adams' Dogs	**ANIMAL AFFAIRS** Barnes Bros. Elephants	Kirk's Dogs
16.		**"MONKEY SHINES"** "Toni"	
17.	Clowns	**ZANY ZEALOTS** Clowns	Clowns
18.		**WONDERS ON WHEELS** The Six Paiges	
19.	Celeste	**"SWING HIGH"** Stanelly	Rozeeta
20.		**EQUINE PRECISION** Blomberg's Liberty Horses	
21.	Clowns	**FOOLS' PARADISE** Clowns	Clowns
22.	Flying Duvards	**"FLYING TRAPEZE"** The Flying Zacchinis	Flying Valentinos
23.		**"WIZARDRY ON THE STEEL THREAD"** The World Famous Wallendas	
24.		**"SKY DANCERS"** Incomparable Betty and Benny Fox	

Ass'st Production Manager............FRED H. KRESSMANN
Arena Director............LEO HAMILTON
Vocal Renditions............MARSILE EDWARDS
Announcements............BOB WHITE
Band Direction............ISADORE CERVONE
Stadium Organist............"Al" MELGARD
Stadium Physician............DR. M. S. CORBETT

— 7 —

The program lists acts from the elephants to the world-famous Wallendas, native German daredevil performers known for their amazing stunts and high-wire acts, in which no safety net was employed. Headlining this particular gala circus was a mammoth $100,000 highly dramatized version of "Alice in Wonderland" with an enchanting set constructed under magic lights.

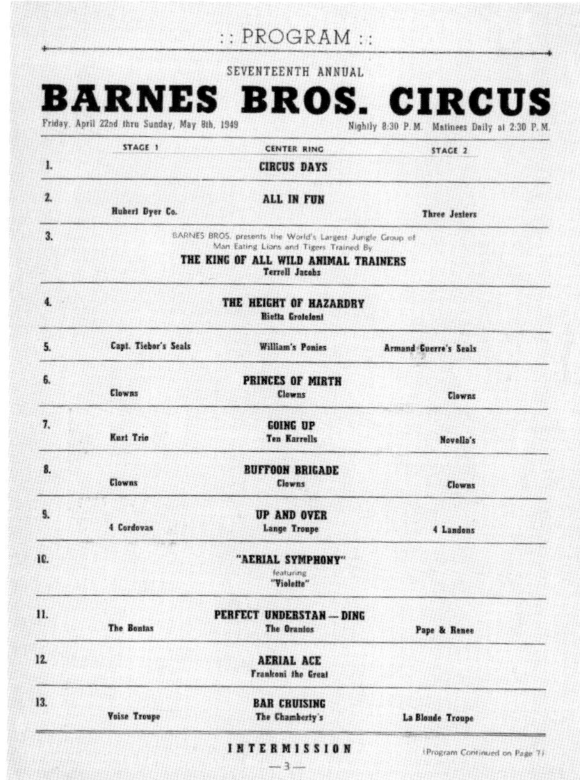

:: PROGRAM ::

SEVENTEENTH ANNUAL

BARNES BROS. CIRCUS

Friday, April 22nd thru Sunday, May 8th, 1949 — Nightly 8:30 P. M. Matinees Daily at 2:30 P. M.

	STAGE 1	CENTER RING	STAGE 2
1.		**CIRCUS DAYS**	
2.	Hubert Dyer Co.	**ALL IN FUN**	Three Jesters
3.		BARNES BROS. presents the World's Largest Jungle Group of Man Eating Lions and Tigers Trained By **THE KING OF ALL WILD ANIMAL TRAINERS** Terrell Jacobs	
4.		**THE HEIGHT OF HAZARDRY** Rietta Grotefent	
5.	Capt. Tiebor's Seals	William's Ponies	Armand Guerre's Seals
6.	Clowns	**PRINCES OF MIRTH** Clowns	Clowns
7.	Kurt Trio	**GOING UP** Ten Karrells	Novello's
8.	Clowns	**BUFFOON BRIGADE** Clowns	Clowns
9.	4 Cordovas	**UP AND OVER** Lange Troupe	4 Landons
10.		**"AERIAL SYMPHONY"** featuring "Violette"	
11.	The Bontas	**PERFECT UNDERSTAN — DING** The Oranios	Pape & Renee
12.		**AERIAL ACE** Frankoni the Great	
13.	Voise Troupe	**BAR CRUISING** The Chamberty's	La Blonde Troupe

INTERMISSION

(Program Continued on Page 7)

— 3 —

The striking images at left and below belong to La Tosca Canestrelli, who was known as "Queen of the Bounding Rope." The daughter of a famed circus family, La Tosca used no supports whatsoever in balancing or performing dance steps and somersaults on the loose bounding rope. Her beauty won her the title of Queen of the Circus from 25 of her peer female performers.

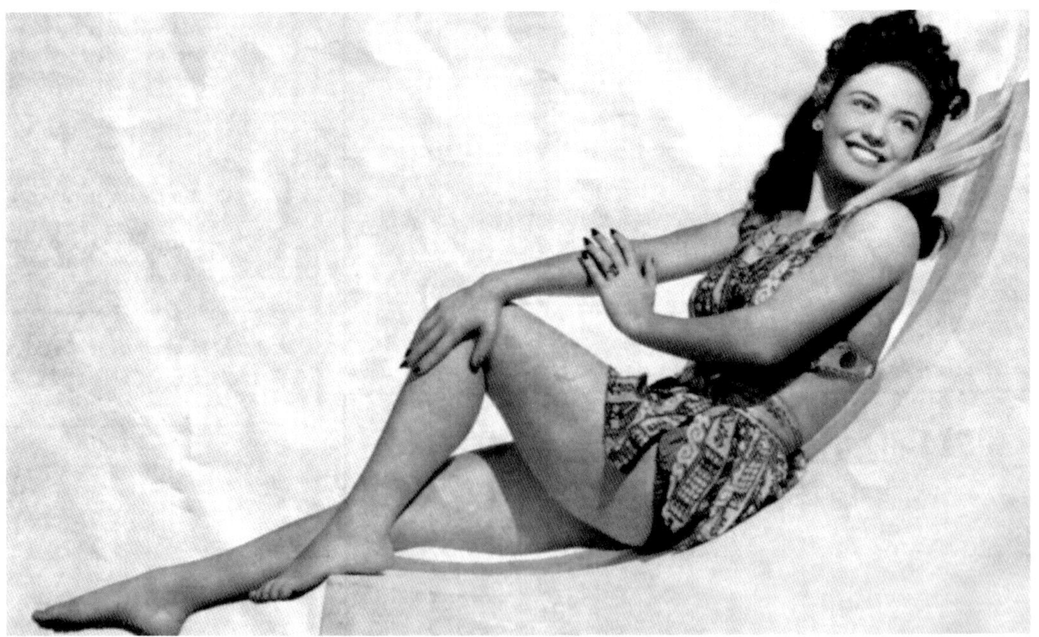

"The Girl in the Moon" featured 1946 sensation Aida, an aerialist who performed her stunts on the wing of a speeding airplane. Reportedly, the plane was hung from the steel beams in the stadium roof.

Trapeze Aerial Star

☆

Elly Ardelty, who has appeared in many Circus movie productions and spent the past few years in Hollywood, returns to the sawdust tents and big circus arenas. Miss Ardelty is one of the foremost aerial swinging trapeze artists in the world and her accomplishments include standing on her head on a swinging bar.

◆

Trapeze Aerial Star Elly Ardelty often performed without the aid of a net and was also featured in a Broadway musical titled "Love Life," in which she played, fittingly, an aerialist. According to circus superstition, females who appeared in the high-wire, flying trapeze, and other stunts that take them 100 feet above the crowds rely on pieces of blue ribbon pinned to their brassieres to keep them from harm. The ribbons are considered good luck charms. Although the image above is approximately 70 years old, the minimalist costume in which she is attired in the image could compete with that of female performers of today.

Terrell Jacobs (pictured in the images above and below) was one of the featured attractions of the circus, gaining fame as the original "Lion King" before the Walt Disney movie of the same name that appeared five decades later. By the time these images were taken, Jacobs had already spent more than three decades in his profession and was credited as the first trainer to make a lion walk a tight wire. A native of Indiana, Jacobs once said, "Lions are essentially one of the smartest of the wild beasts . . . to enter the cage with fear would mean certain disaster for me because the lions would be the first to detect my feelings."

Pictured standing below those five talented pachyderms is Dolly Jacobs, wife of Lion King Terrell Jacobs. An old circus superstition states that the surest of all good luck charms is the hair plucked from the tails of an elephant and touched to the forehead of one of India's sacred cows.

The Eris Troupe, pictured here, was a show business name that dated back to Napoleon. The members were known to leap onto the backs of their running horses and rapidly ascend to a three-person high pyramid. The acrobatic riders were the public's choice of the world's foremost equestrians.

The St. Claire Sisters and performing companion O'Day had a comedic bicycle act that made them prime favorites in their field. More than 10 different wheels were used in their performances, and the image at left reflects only a hint of the swift and graceful acts for which they were known.

Figure skating was a huge draw at Chicago Stadium, as was tennis (mentioned in the advertisement at right).

The acrobatic skating marvels in the image above were known professionally as "The Rollerettes." The four ladies amazed their audiences with swift, acrobatic stunts and unique group formations, both performed with lightning speed.

Too - BIG - For Theaters

OLSEN and JOHNSON

in their

NEW SUPER-COLOSSAL

Musical Revue

"FUNZAPOPPIN"

Three Hours of Rip Roaring Entertainment

Dozens of Gorgeous Dancing Girls

Great Singing Chorus

Carloads of Beautiful Scenery

FUN - FUN - AND MORE FUN

A MILLION DOLLARS WORTH OF LAUGHS

for only

$1.00 Plus Tax

Thousands of Other Seats for $1.50, $1.75, $2.25 Plus Tax. NONE HIGHER

CHICAGO STADIUM

OPENS MAY 13th for 18 Days Only SAT. and SUN. MATINEES

The musical revue *Funzapoppin* offered its patrons three hours of rip-roaring entertainment and was claimed to be too big for theaters. Pictured here is a program page. Olsen and Johnson were two American-born Swedes who met in a band before deciding to strike out together as a vaudeville comedy team. According to author Charles Stumpf, "their 'anything goes' comedy was often greeted with thunderous applause and Olsen and Johnson are remembered to this day as the zaniest of zanies."

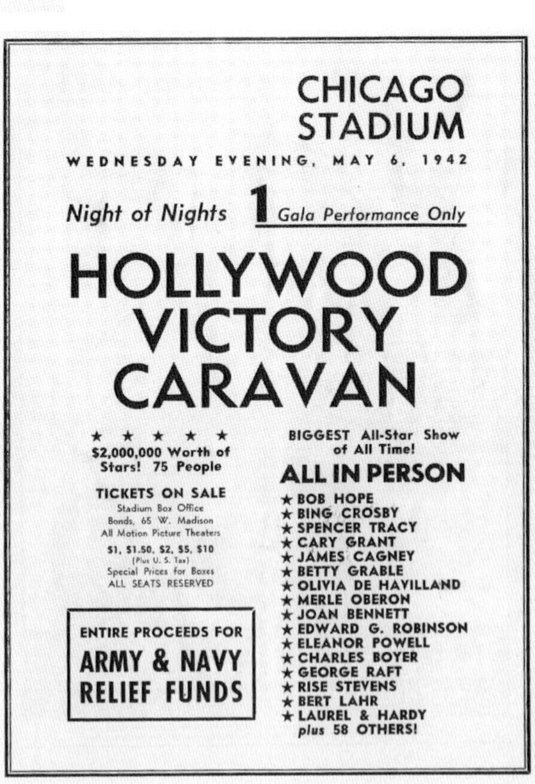

This is an advertisement for Chicago Stadium's only gala performance of the Hollywood Victory Caravan, which netted $800,000 for Army and Navy relief funds and war bonds. Traveling in a special train over three weeks in 1942, the caravan played in 14 cities, performing songs, dances, skits, and ensemble numbers in what the *New York Times* called "the most ambitious money-raising project ever staged by the theatrical world."

Pictured here are Bob Hope and his wife with a young Mickey Rooney following closely behind. Of the Hollywood Victory Caravan, Bob Hope quipped, "Cary Grant, Joan Bennett, Claudette Colbert, Joan Blondell, Charles Boyer, James Cagney . . . It was really a tough trip . . . You were lucky if you could mention your own pictures once every half hour." (Courtesy of author's collection; photograph by Hal McAlpin.)

OPENING HOCKEY GAME • Thurs., Nov. 4th

Chicago Black Hawks vs. New York Americans

PRICES OF ADMISSION

Black Hawk Hockey Games

RESERVED SEATS (All Prices Include Tax)

Box Seats—Main Floor............................$2.50
Mezzanine Seats, 1st 10 Rows Center Sections—
Both Sides 1.75
Remainder of Mezzanine..........................$1.50
Arena Seats, Main Floor........................... 1.50
First Balcony, 3,500 Seats......................... 1.25

NOT RESERVED—Upper Balcony, 3,500 Seats..$0.75. **DOORS OPEN**—Main Floor, 7:30 P. M. Upper Balcony, 6:30 P. M.

TWO TICKET OFFICES

Tickets throughout the season will be on sale at Loop Box Office, 65 W. Madison Street, State 6484, every day except Sunday from 9:30 A. M. to 6:30 P. M., and the Chicago Stadium Grill, 1800 W. Madison Street, Seeley 5300, from 12 (noon) to 8:30 P. M. every day, Sundays included when the Black Hawks play at home. Only season reservations can be had at the Black Hawk's Business Office, 610 N. La Salle Street, (Corner Ontario).

OUR SEASON RESERVATION PLAN

A deposit of $3.75 is required on a $1.25 season reservation
A deposit of $4.50 is required on a $1.50 season reservation
A deposit of $5.25 is required on a $1.75 season reservation
A deposit of $7.50 is required on a $2.50 season reservation

FOR FURTHER INFORMATION PHONE DELaware 2100

A late-1930s game advertisement for the Chicago Black Hawks versus the New York Americans details ticket prices that ranged from a mere $1.25 up to $2.50 for box seats on the main floor.

Emile "The Cat" Francis (born in 1926) began his career in the National Hockey League in 1947 with the Chicago Black Hawks. Reportedly, Francis was the first goaltender to use a first baseman's glove with a cuff added to protect his hand and wrist. Previously, goalies wore the same padded gloves as their teammates. In the image at left, Francis gets taped up prior to his game against the New York Rangers, a team for which he would later play and serve as general manager.

4

POLITICS AND A NEW DEAL

Mayor Thompson don't like my name. Maybe I didn't come over on the Mayflower, but I came as soon as I could.

—future Chicago mayor Anton J. Cermak, 1931

I pledge you, I pledge myself, to a new deal for the American people.

—Franklin D. Roosevelt, Chicago Stadium
1932 Democratic National Convention

Pres. Franklin Delano Roosevelt visited Chicago prior to and during his presidency. (Courtesy of the Franklin D. Roosevelt Library, Hyde Park, New York.)

Pictured here is Pres. Herbert Hoover, who was renominated for his position at the 1932 Republican National Convention, which was held at Chicago Stadium in Chicago from June 14 to June 16, 1932. Although Hoover ran unopposed in his own party, the effects of the 1929 Wall Street Crash and the Great Depression contributed to his falling popularity with voters who lacked confidence in his ability to reverse the economic collapse or deal with prohibition. Pictured below is an interior view of gathering delegates at the Republican National Convention at Chicago Stadium. (Below, courtesy of *Chicago Daily News*.)

Delegates to the National Democratic Party Convention held at Chicago Stadium from June 27 to July 2, 1932, narrowly nominated Roosevelt as their presidential nominee. Pictured above, the Chicago Stadium is all decked out in stars and stripes, ready for the crowd. Below, Franklin D. Roosevelt addresses the assembled delegates. (Both courtesy of Library of Congress.)

Mr. Roosevelt accepted the nomination in person, delivering what has come to be known as the "New Deal for America" speech and promising federal assistance for the millions of Americans hit by the Great Depression. In the political cartoon (inset), Roosevelt appeals to voters who grew tired of Pres. Herbert Hoover during the 1933 presidential elections.

Mayor Anton "Tony" Joseph Cermak was buried on May 13, 1933, in the Bohemian National Cemetery at 5255 North Pulaski Avenue on the north side of Chicago. Cermak was born on May 9, 1873, in Kladno, Austria-Hungary, the present-day Czech Republic. He challenged incumbent Republican mayor "Big Jim" Thompson and won the office on April 7, 1931, becoming Chicago's first Slavic mayor (35th overall) until his assassination by Giuseppe Zangara in 1933.

This March 10, 1933, image shows Mayor Anton J. Cermak's funeral procession on a commercial street in Chicago, Illinois. Cermak was riding in a parade with Pres. Franklin D. Roosevelt at Belmont Park in Miami, Florida, on February 15, 1933, when he was shot by bullets believed to have been meant for President Roosevelt. Cermak died on March 6, 1933. Rumors still exist that the bullets were intended for Cermak, ordered by Al Capone in retaliation for Cermak's alleged involvement in a plot to kill Frank Nitti. (Courtesy of *Chicago Daily News*.)

Pictured above and below are views of flowers making a large cross on the floor of the Chicago Stadium during Mayor Anton J. Cermak's funeral. In the image above, two lines of soldiers stand on either side of Mayor Anton J. Cermak's coffin. In the image below, the cross outlines the stadium floor as mourners view from the seating area. (Both courtesy of *Chicago Daily News*.)

Chicago Stadium hosted the Democratic National Convention from July 19 to July 21, 1944. Pres. Franklin D. Roosevelt was renominated for an unprecedented fourth term while Missouri senator Harry S. Truman was nominated for vice president. FDR's declining health led to his death in April 1945, and Truman became the nation's 33rd president. Pictured above is Harry Truman making his acceptance address upon his nomination for vice president of the United States on July 21, 1944. Pictured at right are, from left to right, Bess Truman, Harry S. Truman, and daughter Margaret Truman at the Democratic National Convention. (Both courtesy of the Harry S. Truman Library, Independence, Missouri.)

Chicago mayor Richard J. Daley (pictured at left) was among John F. Kennedy's key supporters in the 1960 presidential election, providing him with the delegates to win a first-ballot nomination and an overwhelming Chicago vote that delivered Illinois for Kennedy (pictured below). The presidential candidate held his final campaign stop at the stadium, asking a record-breaking crowd to support him on Election Day.

5

The Madhouse on Madison

This place is full of history. Teams come in here and don't like it, this raggedy old place with little locker rooms in the basement, three or four showers, and maybe the hot water doesn't work. I love it. The mystique. It's old-fashioned basketball. I love tradition.

—Michael Jordan on Chicago Stadium

A 1936 magazine advertisement details the Black Hawks' nine-game home schedule. Finishing their 11th season with a home record of 8-13-3 and an overall record of 14-27-7, the Hawks failed to qualify for the play-offs for the first time since 1933, finishing 12 points behind the third-place New York Rangers.

CHICAGO

An early to mid-1960s view of Chicago Stadium's exterior shows a full parking lot and a line of patrons stretching around the block.

Chicago Stadium welcomed old rivals Sugar Ray Robinson (1921–1989) and Jake LaMotta (born July 10, 1921) on February 14, 1951. "The Harlem Dancing Master" (Robinson) and "the Bronx Bull" had met five times previously, and in this match, Robinson defeated a battered but tough LaMotta in 13 rounds to win the world middleweight title. Pictured here is an action shot of the match, which was later dubbed "The St. Valentine's Day Massacre." One news account of the day reported: "Welterweight Champion Ray Robinson wrested the middleweight crown from blood-spattered Jake LaMotta tonight by coming from behind with a savage upper cutting and hooking attack that resulted in a knockout at 2:04 of the thirteenth round." When asked years later how many times he had fought Sugar Ray Robinson, LaMotta responded, "I fought him so many times it's a wonder I don't have diabetes!" Robinson was believed by many to be, pound for pound, the best boxer in the history of the sport.

Pictured here is Jake LaMotta in full boxing stance.

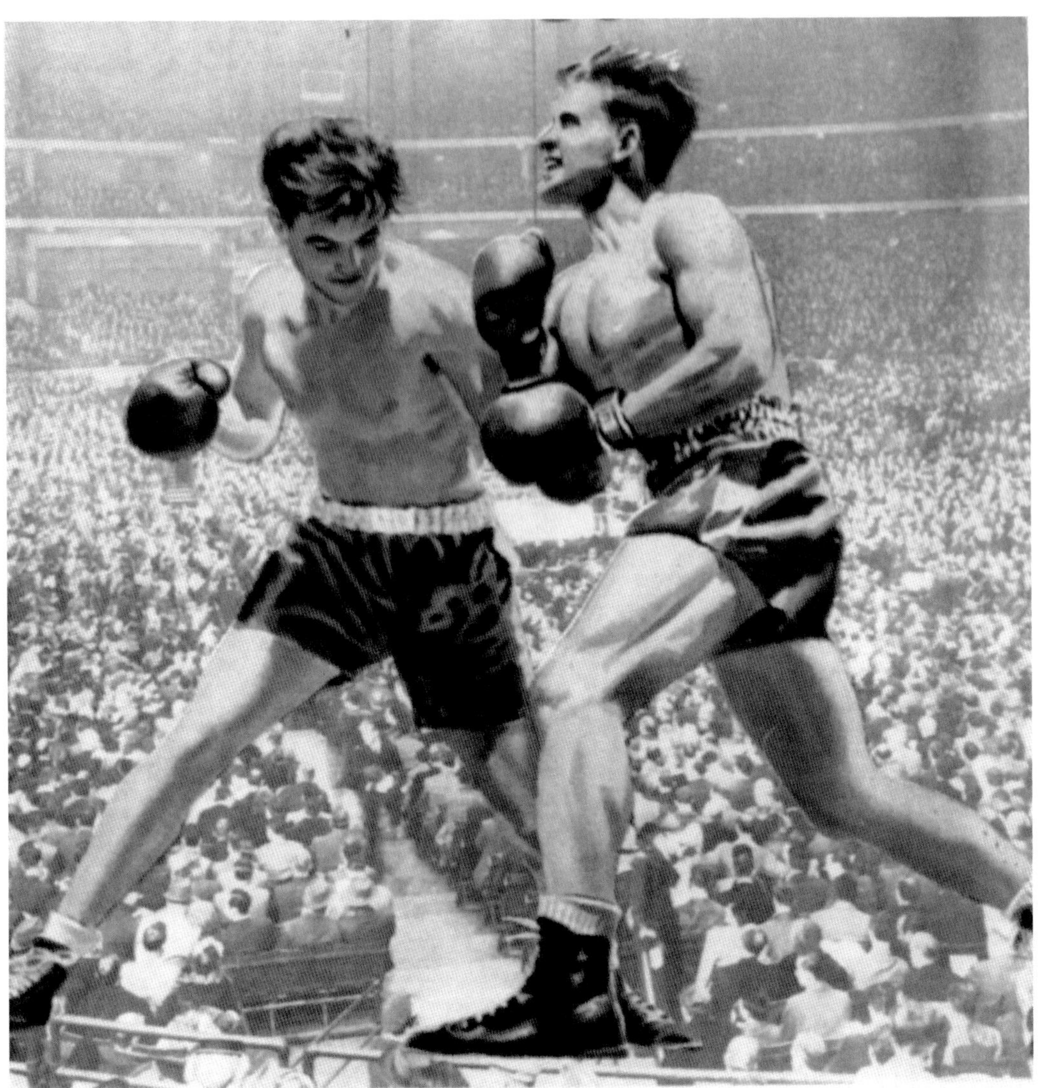

The Chicago Tribune Charities, Inc.

PRESENTS THE

28th Annual Golden Gloves Finals

SANCTIONED BY CENTRAL A. A. U. CHICAGO STADIUM

Official Program 35c **March 10, 1955**

FARACI

Pictured above is a program cover from the March 10, 1955, Chicago Daily Tribune Charities' 28th Annual Golden Gloves Finals held at the stadium. The winners included Eddie Catoe, Eddie Jenkins, Jesse Bowdry, Richard Wall, William Morton, Harry Smith, Donald Eddington, and Tommy Reynolds.

Pictured are some of the participants of the 28th Annual Golden Gloves Finals held at Chicago Stadium. Boxing was one of the early sports that spurred racial integration in professional athletics.

12 28th ANNUAL GOLDEN GLOVES FINALS

GRAND RAPIDS PRESS

Michigan Golden Gloves championships conducted by the Grand Rapids Press were won by boxers from Jackson, Bay City, Kalamazoo, Lansing, and Grand Rapids. The champions, front row, left to right: Gene Foster, 112 pounds; Jim Jabubowski, 118 pounds; Billie Heppner, 126 pounds; Jim McCoy, 135 pounds. Back row: Tommy Johnson, 147 pounds; Jim Wright, 160 pounds; Leonard Murkey, 175 pounds; Clifford Tavenner, heavyweight.

SIOUX CITY JOURNAL AND JOURNAL TRIBUNE

The annual tournament conducted by the Sioux City Journal and Journal Tribune drew amateur boxers from Iowa, Nebraska, and South Dakota. The winners, who fought last week in the Tournament of Champions, are, front row, left to right: James Dye, 112 pounds; Lawrence Brown, 118 pounds; Guido Capri, 126 pounds; Jack Ura, 135 pounds. Back row: Eddie Simmons, coach; Hobart Lonehill, 147 pounds; Dolcar Lamee, 160 pounds; Nick Farmer, 175 pounds; Dale Volberg, heavyweight; Bob Morley, coach.

20 28th ANNUAL GOLDEN GLOVES FINALS

INTERCITY GOLDEN GLOVES

THE Golden Gloves amateur boxing rivalry between Chicago and New York was started in 1928 when the cities tied, 8 bouts to 8, in the Chicago Coliseum. Since then the annual tournaments have been held either in Madison Square Garden or the Chicago Stadium.

Chicago's representatives have won 14 times. They have been defeated six times and there have been seven ties.

Since inception, the Chicago-New York rivalry has become national in scope. Chicago's squad was selected from two score of centers from Cleveland to Los Angeles and from Minneapolis to Texas. New York's territory covers the east.

The record of Intercity Golden Gloves follows:

1928—Chicago, 8; New York, 8.
1929—New York, 11; Chicago, 5.
1930—Chicago, 10; New York, 6.
1931—Chicago, 13; New York, 3.
1932—New York, 12; Chicago, 4.
1933—Chicago, 10; New York, 6.
1934—New York, 9; Chicago, 7.
1935—Chicago, 11; New York, 5.
1936—Chicago, 8; New York, 8.
1937—Chicago, 9; New York, 7.
1938—Chicago, 9; New York, 7.
1939—Chicago 9; New York, 7.
1940—Chicago, 8; New York, 8.
1941—Chicago, 10; New York, 6.
1942—New York, 9; Chicago, 7.
1943—Chicago, 14; New York, 2.
1944—Chicago, 9; New York, 7.
1945—New York, 9; Chicago, 7.
1946—Chicago, 10; New York, 6.
1947—Chicago, 11; New York, 5.
1948—Chicago, 8; New York, 8.
1949—Chicago, 8; New York, 8.
1950—Chicago, 8; New York, 8.
1951—Chicago, 8; New York, 8.
1952—Chicago, 9; New York, 7.
1953—Chicago, 11; New York, 5.
1954—New York, 5; Chicago, 3.

✦

INTERNATIONAL GOLDEN GLOVES

IN 1931 The Chicago Tribune inaugurated Golden Gloves bouts with European nations. France was the first to send its amateur champions to America. The series was broken in 1936 when The Tribune conducted the United States Olympic boxing tournament, but it was resumed the following year against the best boxers in Europe. The World War also interrupted the series.

In 1952 the International Federation was host to Chicago's Golden Gloves champions for the first time and matches were held in Dublin, Paris, Berlin, and Rome. Ten American boys participated according to the new international weight classifications.

The International Golden Gloves record follows:

1931—Chicago, 5; France, 3.
1932—Chicago, 4; Germany, 4.
1933—Chicago, 6; Ireland, 2.
1934—Chicago, 7; Poland, 1.
1935—Chicago, 5; Italy, 3.
1937—Chicago, 4; Europe, 4.
1938—Chicago, 5; Europe, 3.
1939—Europe, 5; Chicago, 3.
1940—Chicago, 4; Europe, 4.
1947—Chicago, 7; Europe, 1.
1948—Chicago, 4; Europe, 4.
1949—Chicago, 5; Europe, 3.
1950—Chicago, 6; Europe, 2.
1951—Chicago, 6; Europe, 2.
1952—Ireland, 6; Chicago, 4.
Chicago, 5; France, 5.
Chicago, 5; Germany, 5.
Chicago, 5; Italy, 5.
1953—Chicago, 6; Europe, 4.
1954—Chicago, 5; Europe, 5.

A detail of the Golden Gloves Champions from 1928 through 1954 lists the victors for each rivalry. The Golden Gloves amateur boxing rivalry began in 1928 when Chicago and New York first met in the Chicago Coliseum, which was the venue precursor to Chicago Stadium. After 1928, the tournaments were held at Chicago Stadium or in New York's Madison Square Garden.

The Catholic Youth Organization inaugurated its annual boxing tournament at the Chicago Stadium on December 4, 1931. As seen here, the event filled the stadium to full capacity, drawing

crowds of 20,000 spectators through the 1930s, 1940s, and 1950s. (Courtesy of Sean Curtin and J.J. Johnston.)

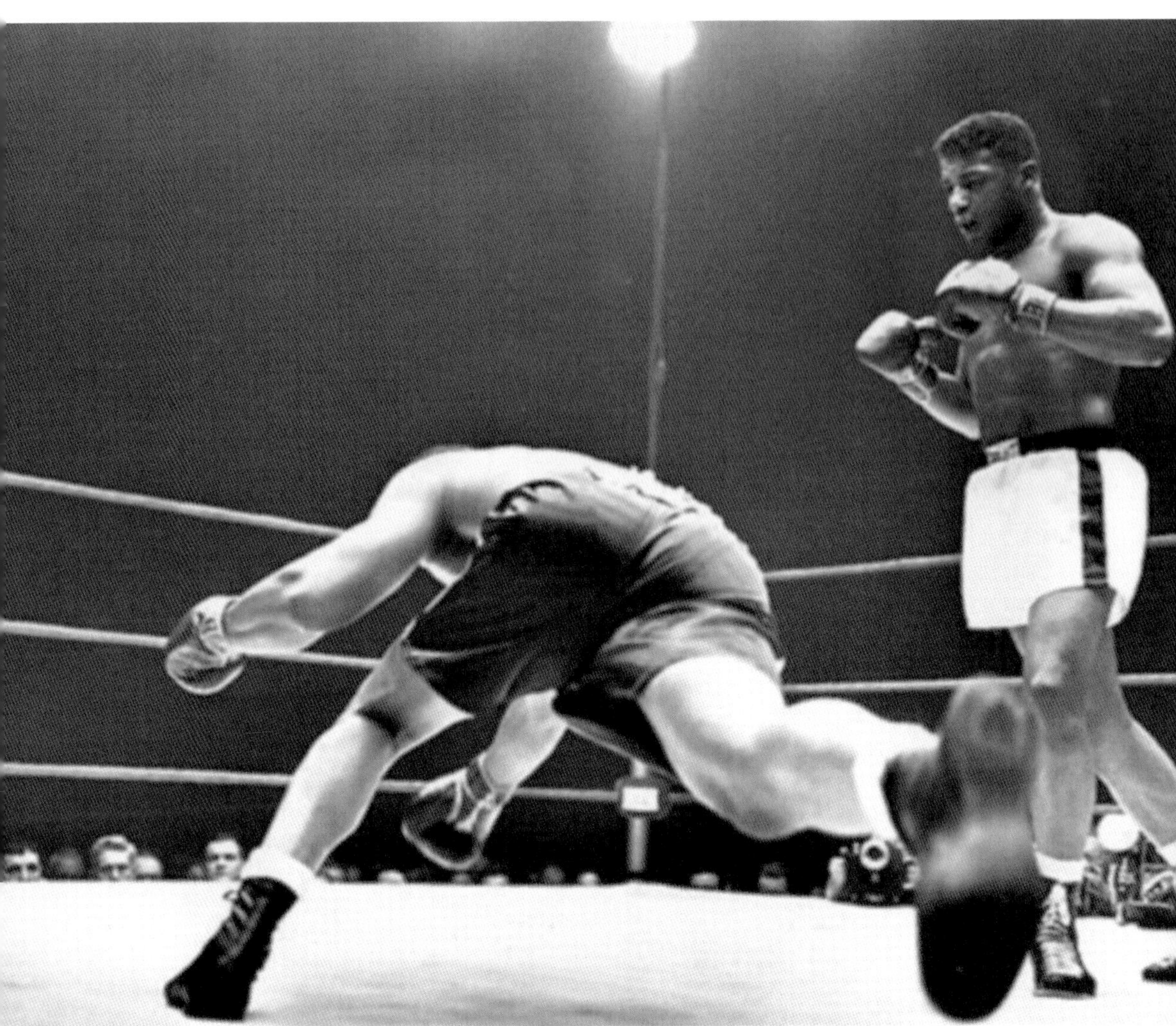

Here, Floyd Patterson watches as Archie Moore crashes to the canvas in the fifth round of their World Heavyweight Championship bout at Chicago Stadium on November 30, 1956. Patterson won the fight to become the world heavyweight champion.

Not all the action took place in the ring. This image was taken at a Chicago Stadium boxing match in 1957.

In this March 19, 1956, photograph, an automatic Skylift fork truck is employed to adjust and measure the crossbar used by pole-vaulters in the Daily News Relays held at Chicago Stadium.

In the 1950s, track meets were a major event and attraction for many fans. A March 27, 1954, program cover for the 18th Annual Chicago Daily News Relays held at Chicago Stadium is shown at left, with participant names for the first four events listed in the image below.

LARRY MARSH anchors Edison Park to victory, 1953.

EDISON PARK City Midget Champs, 1953 L. to r.—MacFarlane, Neuber, Mugg and Marsh.

LANE TECH City High School Relay Champs 1953 L. to r.—Krieger, Duran, Lewis and Marsh.

Event No. 1

City High School Relay

8-11ths of a mile—8 laps. Teams of 4, each man runs 2 laps

DAILY NEWS RELAYS RECORD: 2 minutes, 25.1 seconds, by Du Sable High School, 1942.

1953 DAILY NEWS RELAYS CHAMPION: Lane Tech (Krieger, Duran, Lewis, Marsh) 2:28.6.

AUSTIN	DU SABLE	SCHURZ	LANE TECH
161 J. Hassel	171 C. Ford	166 R. Darnay	156 J. Anderle
162 G. Schneider	172 P. Henley	167 R. Wehr	157 C. Crieger
163 D. Johnson	173 J. Whiteurst	168 R. Uhnavy	158 D. Stuart
164 B. Williams	174 J. Wright	169 J. Viclan	159 G. White
165 R. Salvatore	175 E. Thompson	170 R. Stesch	160 R. Feltz

Won by SCHURZ 2d LANE 3d DuSABLE Time 2:28.06

Event No. 2

Catholic High School Relay

8-11ths of a mile—8 laps. Teams of 4, each man runs 2 laps

DAILY NEWS RELAYS RECORD: 2 minutes, 27.6 seconds, by St. George (Fitzgerald, Leuter, Orth, Hilden), 1951.

1953 DAILY NEWS RELAYS CHAMPION: St. Ignatius (Muchowicz, Tomaskovic, Boyle, Ryan) 2:29.5.

ST. GEORGE	LOYOLA ACD.	ST. IGNATIUS	FENWICK
188 L. DeFrancesca	194 R. Lahart	177 M. Ducar	183 D. Splon
189 P. Dittmer	195 W. O'Keefe	178 R. Boyle	184 C. Boltz
190 E. Shanahan	196 M. O'Connor	179 F. Tomaskovic	185 R. Seneca
191 G. Noonan	197 J. Werner	180 C. Dempsey	186 M. Burke
192 M. Curran	198 G. Sinclair	181 M. Wiltgen	187 R. Scakbal
193 E. Beisinger	199 P. Roberson	182 W. Sclese	

Won by ST IGNATIUS 2d FENWICK 3d ST. GEORGE Time 2:26.0 RECORD

Event No. 3

Junior College Relay

11 laps. Teams of 4, each man runs 440 yards

DAILY NEWS RELAYS RECORD: 3 minutes, 36.2 seconds by Wilson (King, Whitley, Smith, Tounsel), 1952.

1953 DAILY NEWS RELAYS CHAMPION: Wright (Johnson, Giersch, Pinderski, Nesbit) 3:42.

HERZL	WILSON	WRIGHT	NORTH PARK
220 D. Burns	215 C. Durroh	210 G. Pinderski	225 F. Colby
221 J. Fletcher	216 E. Wallis	211 J. Lavin	226 R. Sveiven
222 S. Robinson	217 S. Connor	212 D. Bukowski	227 G. Anderson
223 T. Williams	218 R. Sadder	213 M. Hilden	228 R. Johnson
224 J. Smith	219 J. Ellis	214 J. Nesbit	229 N. Melford

Won by WILSON 2d WRIGHT 3d No. PARK Time 3.37.1

Event No. 4

City Midget Relay

Chicago Elementary School Boys

4-11ths of a mile. Teams of 4, each boy runs 1 lap

DAILY NEWS RELAYS RECORD: 1 minute, 24.8 seconds, by Visitation (Sullivan, Egan, Hanrahan, Sheridan), 1946.

1953 DAILY NEWS RELAYS CHAMPION: Edison Park (MacFarlane, Neubert, Mugg, Marsh) 1:28.9.

OLD TOWN BOYS CLUB	SHOOP PLAYGROUND	EDISON PARK	WABASH YMCA
69 L. V. McKissick	74 R. Howard	64 B. Vineyard	79 R. Collins
70 R. Ramirez	75 R. Kennedy	65 F. Burgbacher	80 W. Collins
71 D. Petersen	76 L. Jones	66 W. Henning	81 C. Simms
72 L. Wallace	77 Joe Howard	67 A. MacFarlane	82 E. Brooks
73 J. Taylor	78 R. Bowers	68 T. Klein	

Won by SHOOP 2d EDISON? 3d WABASH Time 1.27

4

Pictured at right and below are a March 26, 1955, program cover and detail page from the 19th Annual Chicago Daily News Relays. The image below includes samples of event trophies and an introductory welcome from sports editor John P. Carmichael.

Welcome . . . to the Meet of Champs!

As Caesar would have said if he spoke English: "The die is cast!"

Even as you leaf through this program, the events which constitute the 19th Chicago Daily News Relays are assuming form and substance in the guise of 250 standout track stars, many of whom have carried America's colors in past Olympics and will do so again in the 1956 games at Melbourne, Australia.

John P. Carmichael

As they warm up below, against the tension which will send them off and running in this premier indoor presentation of the 1955 season, these past, present and future champions assure you of another enjoyable evening.

They are blue-ribbon performers, culled especially for a blue-ribbon jury.

★ ★ ★

THE BLUE BOOK . . . the "400" of trackdom . . . those running, jumping young giants competing in the free, democratic manner . . . in an event that has become a major tradition in Midwest sports.

This, as always, is an All-American gathering and, as always, with the underlying American purpose to win fairly . . . and, as must be necessary, to lose with the knowledge that every individual effort, is not always good enough in any type of competition.

★ ★ ★

Tonight the Chicago Daily News salutes, with pride, its newest galaxy of stars . . . and also bows to you thousands of fans who, through this patronage, have made it possible for the veterans of all our wars to benefit financially from your presence here.

The best is none too good for you, or for them, and with that thought we get on our marks . . . get set . . . and await the starter's gun which sends another field of Relays champions winging into history . . !

Pictured here is Chicago Bulls point guard Norm Van Lier III (April 1, 1947–February 26, 2009), who spent the majority of his NBA career with the Chicago Bulls. Nicknamed "Stormin' Norman" for his tenacity and aggression, Van Lier was one of the most popular Bulls players of the 1970s.

Pictured in this photograph is Glenn Hall (born October 3, 1931), who played for the Chicago Black Hawks from 1957 until 1967. Nicknamed "Mr. Goalie," Hall hardly missed a game or an award in his 18 seasons with the National Hockey League. Hall is credited with having developed an effective style of goaltending that is referred to today as "the butterfly style."

After a two-decade-plus dry spell on the ice, the Chicago Black Hawks returned to past glory as the 1961 Stanley Cup Champions following a 5-1 victory over the Detroit Red Wings. In a *Chicago Tribune* article dated April 16, 1961, reporter Bob Foltman wrote, "After a long sentence in hockey Siberia, the Black Hawks emerged in the 1960–61 season as an almost perfect blend of youth and experience, backstopped by peerless goalie Glenn Hall, the 'quiet, calm, nerveless knight of the nets,' as the Tribune described him. Stan Mikita and Bobby Hull, the 'Golden Jet,' had yet to reach their prime but were already forces in the old six-team National Hockey League." Pictured above is the team photograph at the end of that season.

Goaltender Denis Emile DeJordy (born in Canada on November 12, 1938) was called up to the Black Hawks in the 1962–1963 season. His first NHL game was on November 8, 1962, when he replaced Glenn Hall. By 1964, DeJordy was the Hawks' principal goaltender.

Dennis Hull was often overshadowed by his superstar brother Bobby and, later, his nephew Brett. Yet Dennis, about five years younger than Bobby, was a star in his own right and was always a popular player with the Black Hawks. Many thought his slap shot was actually harder than Bobby's. He played 14 seasons in the NHL, all but the last with the Black Hawks. He retired after the 1977–1978 season. Dennis Hull scored 303 goals in his NHL career, playing in 959 games. He also had 351 assists. He scored 33 play-off goals in 104 games. In 1972, he played for Team Canada in the Summit Series against the Soviet Union. He played in five NHL All-Star Games.

This image from February 24, 1972, shows Chicago Black Hawks defenseman Keith Magnuson (second from the left) landing a punch over the shoulder of linesman Ron Finn to the back of the Buffalo Sabres' Tracy Pratt. Bob McLaren (far left) rushes to assist after Magnuson had pushed him to the ice moments earlier. Viewing the spectacle are Rick Martin (No. 7) and Black Hawks right wing Jim Pappin. Sadly, Magnuson was killed in an automobile accident in Ontario on December 15, 2003. The Blackhawks retired his number in 2008. (Courtesy of United Press International.)

Grant Mulvey was a first-round pick of the Black Hawks, joining the team as an 18-year-old rookie in the 1974–1975 season. He played eight full seasons for the Black Hawks. In October 1982, he suffered a knee injury in a game against Detroit, effectively ending his career.

After playing 13 games for the Montreal Canadiens in the 1968–1969 season, Tony Esposito was claimed by the Black Hawks in the intra-league draft in June 1969 and was a fixture in the Hawks' net for the next 15 seasons. The popular goalie was a six-time all-star inducted into the Hockey Hall of Fame in 1988. "Tony O," as he was known by fans in Chicago, revolutionized goaltending by standing with his legs open. He was known for making spectacular saves. He is the younger brother of Phil Esposito, who played four seasons with the Black Hawks but was gone before Tony arrived. Phil went on to be a hall-of-fame goal scorer for the Bruins and Rangers in an 18-season career. Both Esposito brothers were durable; several times each led the league in games played.

Hockey Hall of Famer Robert Marvin "Bobby" Hull (born January 3, 1939, in Point Anne, Ontario, Canada), pictured above (No. 9) and on the opposite page, joined the Chicago Black Hawks in 1957 at the age of 18. Standing only 5 feet and 10 inches tall with a playing weight of 185 pounds, Hull's electrifying style would make him one of hockey's first international superstars and, arguably, the National Hockey League's marquee star of the 1960s.

In the 1972 image here, a beaming Bobby Hull holds up the puck with which he scored his 600th NHL career goal in a game against the Boston Bruins. With only two minutes and 26 seconds remaining in the game, Hull helped the Black Hawks to a 5-5 tie. (Courtesy of United Press International.)

Hull's playing career spanned from 1957 to 1980. He was inducted into the Hockey Hall of Fame in 1983.

Pictured at left and below is Stan Mikita (born May 20, 1940), who spent his entire career with the Chicago Black Hawks and is widely regarded as the best center of the 1960s. Like his teammate Bobby Hull, Mikita was a formidable player who helped the Black Hawks win the Stanley Cup in 1961. His playing career spanned from 1959 to 1980, and he was admitted into the Hockey Hall of Fame in 1983.

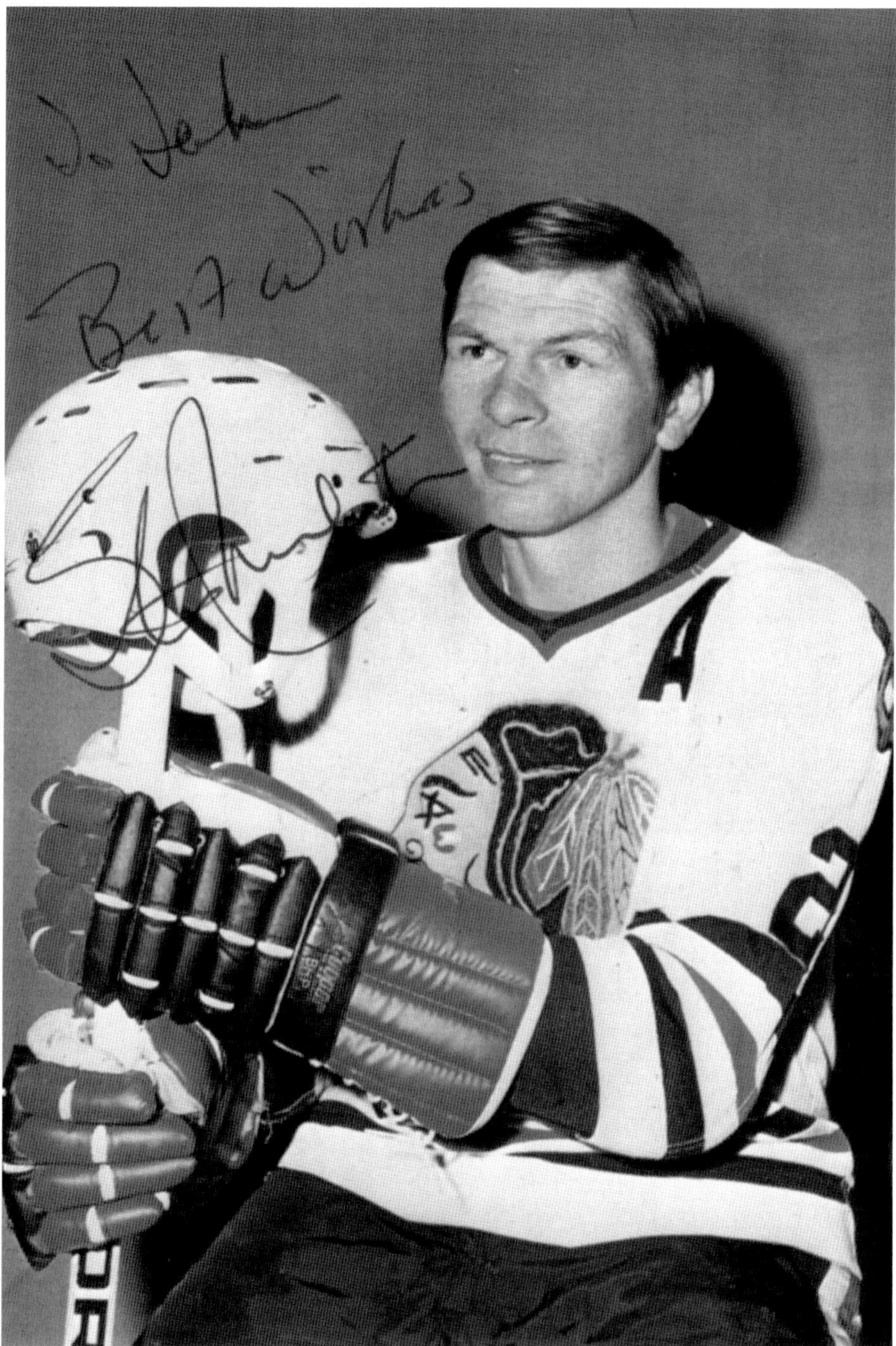

In the 1970 *The Chicago Black Hawks Story*, author George Vass quoted coach Billy Reay on Stan Mikita: "I've seen most of the good centers who have been around for the last 25 years or so. I have to say I have never seen a better center . . . none of them could do all the things that a center has to do as well as Stan does. And very few of them came close to being as smart as he is. That's his greatest asset. He's smart. He's about the brightest hockey player I've ever seen."

Above is an October 16, 1988, image of Dennis Savard, who played in the National Hockey League from 1980 to 1997 and was elected to the Hockey Hall of Fame in 2000. He has also served as head coach of the Chicago Blackhawks. Savard began his career during the 1980–1981 NHL season, in which he had three assists in his first game. He was known for his trademark move, the "Savardian Spin-o-rama," which entailed Savard whirling around with the puck in a full rotation, allowing him to defeat defenders and goaltenders alike.

Darcy Rota, born in Vancouver in 1953, was a first-round draft pick of the Black Hawks in 1973. He played with the Black Hawks for six seasons, jumping right in his rookie season and playing in 74 games and scoring 21 goals. Rota played left wing for the Black Hawks and scored 117 goals in his six seasons in Chicago. In his early years with the Black Hawks, Rota played on a line with legends Stan Mikita and Cliff Karroll.

Chicago Stadium was a great venue for basketball. This 1950s advertisement hypes the "World Series of Basketball," a competition between college All-Americans and the Harlem Globetrotters.

32 28th ANNUAL GOLDEN GLOVES FINALS

A SPORTS MUST!!!

Sunday, April 3rd

MATINEE GAME—2:30 P. M.

THE WORLD SERIES OF BASKETBALL

1955 COLLEGE ALL-AMERICANS

(The 11 outstanding senior players of current season)

vs.

FABULOUS HARLEM GLOBETROTTERS

TICKETS NOW . . . $1.50 - $2.50 - $3.50 - $4.75 (Including Tax)

CHICAGO STADIUM
1800 West Madison

BOND'S
State and Jackson

Or By Mail to THE CHICAGO STADIUM

CHICAGO BULLS 1967-68

Shown here is a 1967–1968 team photograph of the Chicago Bulls, the first season in which they played at Chicago Stadium. The first Bulls game at the stadium took place on October 17, 1967, when the Los Angeles Lakers defeated the Bulls 107-105. Coached by Johnny "Red" Kerr, the 1967–1968 playing year was the Bulls' second season of the franchise in the NBA.

In this image dated February 1, 1970, Cincinnati Royals player Luther Rackley (No. 22) leaps high over the Chicago Bulls' Tom Boerwinkle (No. 18) and Chet Walker at Chicago Stadium. The Bulls claimed a victory, though, with a final score of 115-108. (Courtesy of United Press International.)

In this photograph from December 22, 1976, the Supersonics' Willie Norwood (right) and the Bulls' Cliff Pondexter grapple for the ball during the first half of the game. Chicago beat Seattle 103-101 in double overtime. (Courtesy of United Press International.)

Pictured here is "His Airness," Michael Jordan, who was born on February 17, 1963, in Brooklyn, New York. Jordan joined the NBA's Chicago Bulls in 1984 after emerging as a standout at the University of North Carolina at Chapel Hill, where he led the Tar Heels to a national championship in 1982. Jordan was a league sensation who quickly became known as one of the best—if not the best—player in the NBA.

Jordan won his first NBA championship with the Bulls in 1991, following up this achievement with titles in 1992 and 1993 for a three-peat.

Scottie Pippen was born September 25, 1965, in Hamburg, Arkansas, one of 12 children. His biography notes that he is most remembered for his time with the Chicago Bulls and that he was instrumental in their six NBA championships and the team's record 1995–1996 season of 72 wins. Michael Jordan and Pippen transformed the Bulls into a vehicle for popularizing the NBA around the world during the 1990s.

This photograph was taken at Chicago Stadium during the 1992 NBA play-offs between the Chicago Bulls and the New York Knicks. Note Michael Jordan at mid-court, right as the ball is tipped.

Pictured above and below is the famed 3,663-pipe Barton organ that helped Chicago Stadium earn the nickname "the Madhouse on Madison" by inspiring the loud, rising noise of Stadium fans. Legend has it that in the early days of the stadium, when staff organist Al Melgard was on duty at the console, an unpopular decision following a boxing match resulted in a riot. Melgard played a rousing version of the "National Anthem," which helped quell the rioters and also shattered light bulbs and windows in the cavernous stadium. Expecting dismissal because of the damage, Melgard was instead rewarded with the promise of a lifetime position.

Pictured here is a unique view of the Barton pipe organ nestled in the loft of Chicago Stadium. The image was taken on April 8, 1994, just before the Blackhawks took on the St. Louis Blues. Standing ready to lead the crowd in the "Star-Spangled Banner" is vocalist Wayne Messmer. Later that evening, after the game, Messmer was mugged and shot in the throat while outside Hawkeye's Bar and Grill. Fortunately, Messmer survived and is a successful businessman today.

Following in the footsteps of Frank Sinatra, Elvis Presley, and rock band KISS, Led Zeppelin was among the many musical performances that took place during the stadium's 60-plus-year history. Pictured here, Led Zeppelin played three shows at the venue in 1975 during their 10th North American tour. Two years later, in the spring of 1977, the group played four additional shows at the stadium. Two more were scheduled for later in the tour but were cancelled due to the death of Robert Plant's son.

6

Remember the Roar!

At that moment I knew, surely and clearly, that I was witnessing perfection. He stood before us, suspended above the earth, free from all its laws like a work of art, and I knew, just as surely and clearly, that life is not a work of art, and that the moment could not last.

—Norman MacLean
A River Runs Through It, 1976

Pictured here is the famous bronze statue of basketball legend Michael Jordan that stands outside the United Center. The Norman MacLean quote above is inscribed at its base.

Pictured above and below is the final Chicago Blackhawks game schedule at Chicago Stadium for the 1993–1994 season. In that final season at the stadium, box seats cost $65, a bargain by today's price standards.

September '93

SUN	MON	TUES	WED	THUR	FRI	SAT
19 DET	20	21 @DET	22 @WINN	23	24	25 @ST.L.
26 ST.L.	27	28	29	30		

October '93

SUN	MON	TUES	WED	THUR	FRI	SAT
					1 WINN	2 @SJ
3	4	5		7	8	9 SC TOR
	11	12 SC DAL	13		15	16 SC WINN
17		19	20		22	
24	25		27		29	30 SC PITTS

November '93

SUN	MON	TUES	WED	THUR	FRI	SAT
	1		3		5	6
	8	9	10		12	13 SC TOR
	15	16	17	18 SC FLO	19	20 SC TAMP
21	22	23	24 SC EDM	25	26 SC CALG	27
28	29 SC VANC	30				

December '93

SUN	MON	TUES	WED	THUR	FRI	SAT
			1	2	3	4 SC NJ
5	6	7 SC ST.L.	8	9	10	11 SC BOS
	13	14	15 SC DAL	16	17	18 SC PHIL*
	20	21 SC DET	22		24	25
26 SC ST.L.		28	29 SC WINN	30		

January '94

SUN	MON	TUES	WED	THUR	FRI	SAT
						1
	3	4 SC DAL	5		7	8 SC WASH*
	10		12		14	15 SC NYI
	17	18	19	20	21	22 All-Star Game in NY
23	24	25 SC DET	26		28	
30	31 SC OTT					

February '94

SUN	MON	TUES	WED	THUR	FRI	SAT
		1	2 SC VANC	3	4 SC EDM	5
6 SC ANA*	7	8 SC SJ IN SC	9 SC LA	10	11 SC SJ	12
13 SC SJ*	14 SC CALG	15	16		18 SC WINN	19
	21	22	23		25 SC BUFF	26
	28					

March '94

SUN	MON	TUES	WED	THUR	FRI	SAT
		1	2		4	5
	7	8 SC ANA IN PX	9 SC LA	10	11 SC ANA	12
	14 SC QUE	15	16 SC MONT	17	18 SC NYR	19
	21	22 SC DET	23		25	26
	28	29	30 SC HART			

April '94

SUN	MON	TUES	WED	THUR	FRI	SAT
					1	2
	4	5 SC ST.L.	6	7		9
	11	12 SC TOR	13		15	16

Pictured above is a scene from the Blackhawks' final season in Chicago Stadium.

Lite
Gatorade
HAWKS
0
PLR PTY
20:00
PERIOD
1
LEAFS
0
PLR PTY
REMEMBER
THE ROAR!
1929
1994
SHOTS
Enjoy Coca-Cola
Winston
SportsChannel
Miller Genuine Draft

Players from the Chicago Blackhawks and the Toronto Maple Leafs stand for the opening of the final game at Chicago Stadium.

Jeremy Roenick scores the last goal for the Blackhawks in one of the final games at Chicago Stadium. Of his experience in Chicago Stadium, Roenick is quoted as saying, "It was indescribable to be there. The experience was second to none. We always thought we had a two-goal lead there before coming out of the tunnel. If you didn't have goose bumps, and the hair wasn't standing up on the back of your neck, then you better get your pulse taken because you weren't alive."

The final hockey game at Chicago Stadium was played on April 28, 1994. The Blackhawks lost to the Toronto Maple Leafs 1-0, eliminating them from the Stanley Cup Playoffs. In the image, players from both teams shake hands at the game's end.

According to one website about Chicago Stadium, it was the very last NHL-used facility to have an analog, dial-type, large, four-sided clock for timekeeping during professional hockey games. That clock eventually was replaced by a four-sided scoreboard with a digital clock, which was replaced by another with a color electronic message board. In the image above, the four-sided analog scoreboard is taken down and removed before the stadium's ultimate demolition.

In this image taken on September 9, 1994, Michael Jordan kneels down to kiss the Chicago Bulls logo at half-court in the last basketball game at the Chicago Stadium. Jordan came out of his first retirement to play this charity game. (Creative Commons: Jelipe.)

A new arena opened for business on August 18, 1994. In the image above, Chicago Stadium stands next to its replacement, the United Center. The plan to build the arena was carried out by the late Bill Wirtz and Jerry Reinsdorf, owners of the Chicago Blackhawks and the Chicago Bulls, respectively. Corporate sponsor United Airlines pays about $1.8 million per year until 2014 for naming rights at the United Center, according to ESPN's website.

Pictured above is the electronic scoreboard with one final message to fans of the once-great stadium: "Remember the Roar."

Passersby witness the demolition of Chicago Stadium in March 1995. This view was taken from United Center just prior to a Blackhawks game.

In the 2010 images above and below, a large parking lot sits adjacent to United Center where Chicago Stadium once stood.

Pictured at right is a cover detail from the first program for the Chicago Bulls in their new venue at United Center. Below is an interior map detail of United Center's seating levels.

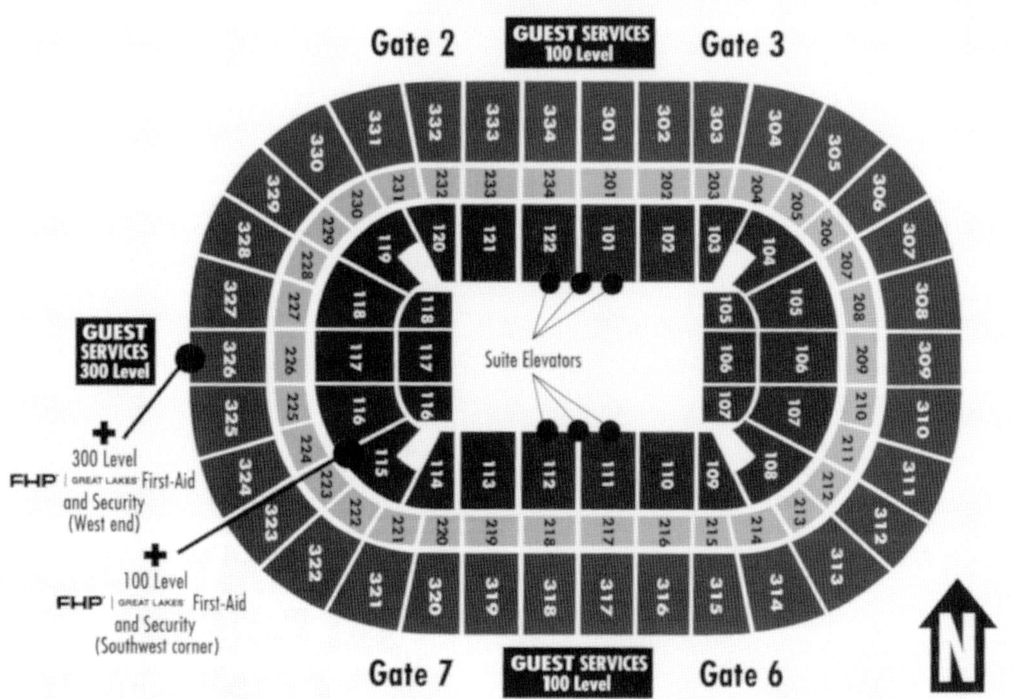

Located at 1901 West Madison Street and commonly referred to as "the UC" or "the House that Jordan Built," United Center was built at a construction cost of $175 million, more than 17 times the cost of building its predecessor, the Chicago Stadium. The project broke ground in April 1992 and opened on August 18, 1994. The current owners and operators of United Center are Rocky Wirtz (son of Bill Wirtz) and Jerry Reinsdorf.

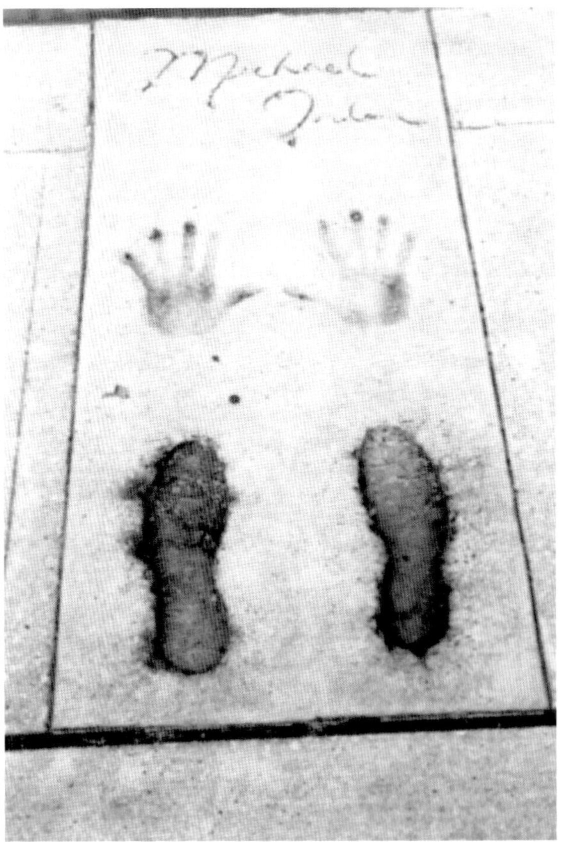

Pictured is a slab of concrete bearing the impressions of Michael Jordan's hands and feet near the Michael Jordan statue (see opposite page) in front of United Center.

Featured on this page are images of the Michael Jordan statue that graces the front entrance to United Center. In 1993, Chicago Bulls vice president Steve Schanwald was directed by Jerry Reinsdorf to locate a sculptor who could pay homage to the greatest living basketball player in history. In January 1994, according to the United Center website, the husband-and-wife team of Omri and Julie Rotblatt-Amrany of Highland Park, Illinois, were commissioned to design and create a statue of the Bulls superstar that would stand forever at the entrance to United Center. Cast in bronze, the statue measures 12 feet tall (17 feet from top to bottom) and weighs 2,000 pounds. Reportedly, the Michael Jordan statue is one of Chicago's most popular tourist attractions.

Pictured here is the 75th anniversary commemorative sculpture of the Chicago Blackhawks located across the street from United Center. The sculpture was unveiled on October 12, 2000. Created by renowned sculptor Erik Blome, the five-foot-tall bronze work and monumental black granite pedestal features six life-size hockey players representative of different eras in the NHL's past. The pedestal features 800 sandblasted names of every hockey player to ever have played for the team between 1926 and the present.

7

SURROUNDING ENVIRONS—CHICAGO'S WEST SIDE STORY

Right now my sister and I are watching West Madison burn down. Pulaski and Roosevelt have already gone. All we can do is sit and watch the smoke, clouds, and flames, and the troops move in.

—Eyewitness account of the 1968 Chicago riots
the morning after Dr. Martin Luther King Jr.'s death

In April 1968, Rev. Martin Luther King Jr. was assassinated, and the West Side of Chicago erupted into the worst race riot since those on the South Side in 1919. Entire commercial blocks were leveled, and the looting, arson, and violence eventually consumed an entire 28-block stretch of West Madison Street. In the image above, rioters clash with Chicago police in one of the numerous scenes that would serve as a catalyst for many neighborhood residents forever leaving the city's West Side.

Hull House was cofounded in 1889 by Jane Addams and Ellen Gates Starr on the Near West Side of Chicago. The settlement house immediately opened its doors to the recently arrived European emigrants. The Hull House Museum reports that the greater Hull House neighborhood on Chicago's Near West Side was a mix of various ethnic groups that had immigrated to Chicago. There was no discrimination of race, language, creed, or tradition for those who entered the doors of the Hull House, and every person was treated with respect.

Pictured above in the distance from United Center is Rush University Medical Center, a not-for-profit health care, education, and research enterprise. Rush is the largest nongovernmental employer on Chicago's West Side and is the 20th largest private-sector employer in Chicago, with more than 8,000 employees and a payroll of more than $500 million.

Pictured next to the former Sears Tower is a rent-controlled senior housing complex catering to neighborhood residents within a few blocks of United Center's front doors.

Although the surrounding area of Chicago's West Side near United Center reveals the potential for gentrification as young professionals begin migrating to some of the newer condominium developments, evidence of poverty still abounds, as shown in this view of a dilapidated two-story home surrounded by uncut grass and the adjacent four-flat apartment building weathered by the passing of time.

Pictured here is one of the many city cameras that were installed at various intersections throughout Chicago to record evidence of crimes in progress and red-light scofflaws.

One restaurant staple that has remained on Chicago's West Side since its inception is the famous Billy Goat Tavern of "Cheezborger, cheezborger, cheezborger" *Saturday Night Live* fame. According to the restaurant's website, the original Billy Goat Tavern location was "born" in 1934 when Greek emigrant William "Billy Goat" Sianis purchased the Lincoln Tavern. Sianis bought the tavern for $205 with a check that bounced but was later repaid with sales from the first weekend. The tavern was located across from the Chicago Stadium and attracted many sports fans.

Pictured outside the restaurant are neighborhood regulars James Ross (left) and friend William Howard, fresh from picking up a to-go order.

At Chicago's famous Billy Goat Tavern, customers can prepare their own "cheezborger." It is served open-face and still steaming from the grill. Patrons are cautioned, as the sign reads, to "enter at your own risk."

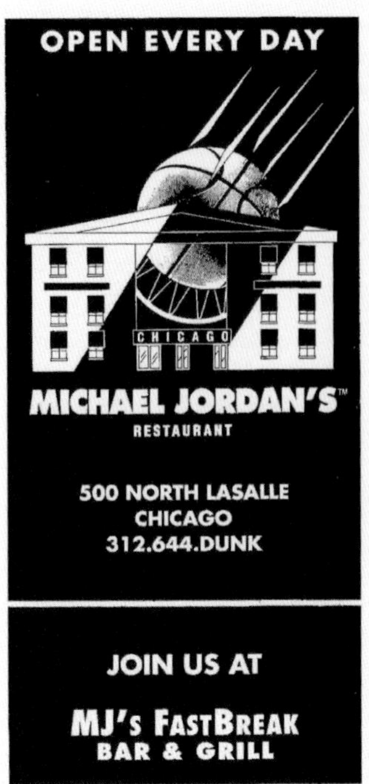

An advertisement page from the first Chicago Bulls program at United Center in the early 1990s offers several culinary choices for before or after the game. Note, however, that the locations remain outside of the immediate sphere of the West Side, harbored more safely in prime downtown areas or the upwardly mobile and gentrified areas known as "Bucktown" and "River North."

Designated a Chicago landmark on January 21, 1982, the First Baptist Congregational Church is located on North Ashland Avenue on the Near West Side, close to United Center. The church was built between 1869 and 1871 by Gurdon P. Randall. According to the church's website, it was originally known as the Union Park Congregational Church. The architecture is Gothic in style, and the building is constructed of masonry and limestone.

What would Chicago be without the world famous L, or elevated train? Pictured above Peoples Stadium Parking is the Chicago Transit Authority's Green Line making its way to the Ashland Avenue stop.

Participants are eager for the sold-out 2010 Blackhawks Training Camp Festival, a marquee event that allows a standing-room-only crowd inside the United Center to watch the Blackhawks' first day of on-ice practices and scrimmages.

Pictured here is the finish line during preparation for the festival's outdoor activities, which include a 5-kilometer walk and run and a 10-kilometer inline skate named "the Mad Dash to Madison." During the 2010 Blackhawks Training Camp Festival, ticket holders could catch a glimpse of the famous Stanley Cup, which was on display in the United Center.

Participants enjoy some rough-and-tumble, three-on-three street hockey.

"Mad Dash on Madison" 5-kilometer participants Jen Patterson (left) and WIND radio personality Amy Jacobson are all smiles and ready for a run as they pose for a prerace photograph.

Pictured above, from left to right, are Chicago Blackhawks fans Dennis Scherer, Alex Scherer, and Chris Tuscan on hand for the day's events and a glimpse at the Stanley Cup. Scherer reminisced that, as a youngster, he watched Stan Mikita play at the old Chicago Stadium. Pictured at left, runners warm up for the 5-kilometer race, including one participant who is paying homage to Chief Black Hawk in full Indian headdress.

Sgts. Milton Flores and Tamba Folley of the 2nd Battalion, 24th Marines Company, 4th Marine Division, offer festival participants a closer inspection of the MK3 Humvees all-terrain combat assault vehicles. According to Flores, the Humvee seats five marines and is used for mobile patrols and convoys.

Chicago band Spoken Four performs a range of hits from the past four decades to entertain this year's festival attendees.

Scenes from outside United Center include the famous "hockey tree" framing the parking lot.

This plaque is set in concrete as a memorial for Chicago Stadium.

"Remember the Roar."

BIBLIOGRAPHY

Cohen, Adam, and Elizabeth Taylor. *American Pharaoh: Mayor Richard J. Daley—His Battle for Chicago and the Nation*. New York: Little, Brown and Company, 2000.

Ferrell, Robert H. *Choosing Truman: The Democratic Convention of 1944*. Columbia, MO: University of Missouri Press, 1994.

Gottfried, Alex. *Boss Cermak of Chicago: A Study of Political Leadership*. Seattle: University of Washington Press, 1962.

Greenland, Paul R. *Hockey Chicago Style: The History of the Chicago Blackhawks*. Champaign, IL: Sagamore Publishing, 1995.

Grossman, James R., Ann Durkin Keating, and Janice L. Reiff, eds. *The Encyclopedia of Chicago*. Chicago: University of Chicago Press, 2004.

Halberstam, David. *Playing for Keeps: Michael Jordan and the World He Made*. New York: Random House, 1999.

Hayner, Don, and Tom McNamee. *The Stadium: 1929–1994, the Official Commemorative History of the Chicago Stadium*. Chicago: Performance Media, 1994.

Picchi, Blaise. *The Five Weeks of Giuseppe Zangara: The Man Who Would Assassinate FDR*. Chicago: Academy Chicago, 1998.

Seligman, Amanda. *Block by Block: Neighborhoods and Public Policy on Chicago's West Side*. Chicago: University of Chicago Press, 2005.

Tabbert, Christopher. *Heydays: Great Stories in Chicago Sports*. Arlington Heights, IL: Bristol and Lynden, 2009.

Vass, George. *The Chicago Black Hawks Story*. Chicago: Follett, 1970.

Consistent with our mission to preserve history on a local level, this book was printed in South Carolina on American-made paper and manufactured entirely in the United States. Products carrying the accredited Forest Stewardship Council (FSC) label are printed on 100 percent FSC-certified paper.